You're Not in MOM'S KITCHEN Anymore!

college cooking for THE DORMING GOURMET

BY GARRY PASTORE

EDITED BY GINA LaGUARDIA

COLLEGE BOUND MAGAZINE

Published by:

2071 Clove Road, Suite 206

Staten Island, NY 10304

(718) 273-5700

Creative Direction: Giulio Rammairone
Cover & Book Design: Suzanne Massaro
Clay Buffet: Image Club/Object Gear

You're Not in MOM'S KITCHEN Anymore!

college cooking for THE DORMING GOURMET

BY GARRY PASTORE

EDITED BY GINA LaGuardia

COLLEGE BOUND MAGAZINE

Since 1987, Ramholtz Publishing, Inc. has been completely in touch with the teenage college-bound audience. With almost ten years in the industry of publishing, *College Bound Magazine*– the most widely read, most popular student advice magazine *ever*– has seen its regional circulation double to 100,000, and its national issue become the highlight of homeroom sessions. That's where over 725,000 of the nation's teens get the magazine's Annual National Edition each February.

And, because teens can't get enough of this straight-at-ya', helpful and exciting information dissemination *(SAT word here!)*, *CollegeBound.NET* at *http://www.cbnet.com* has become one of the coolest clicks in cyberspace! It offers tons of interactive departments, features, polls, surveys, contests, games, and more! High school seniors can even enter *College Bound Magazine's* Student of the Year scholarship contest and win big prizes right on-line!

COLLEGE BOUND *MAGAZINE*

GARRY PASTORE

AUTHOR

Garry was born and raised in New York City as the middle child in a family of six. Always craving the attention of others, and usually starved for affection, Garry began his career in entertaining at an early age— even if it meant getting in trouble as the class clown!

He became a singer in a rock 'n' roll band in his latter years of high school. Due to the tenacity of his drama teacher, he was eventually persuaded to cut his hair and get involved in "tamer" school productions. After landing the lead in Tottenville High School's "West Side Story", his stage and film career began.

Over the years, as a source of income, he dabbled in the restaurant business. He began working as a dishwasher and busboy while in high school and eventually became more and more intrigued with the idea of becoming a chef. As most college freshmen, he wavered many a time with proclamations of his major— the thought crossed his mind about going to medical school, but 10 more years of teachers and homework didn't particularly appeal to him. Needless to say, culinary school became his most likely and enjoyable option.

Upon graduation as a chef in 1981, he moved to Manhattan, NY and worked at various establishments while continuing to pursue his career in the entertainment business. He lucked out when he landed a job at the famous "Silver Palate" eatery on Columbus Avenue. It was there that he got the chance to whip up some meals for the late Jaqueline Kennedy-Onassis and other such lavish luminaries. He still maintained a place in the entertainment spotlight by landing parts in quite a number of films. In addition, he took up screenplay writing as a hobby, and wrote, produced, and directed an off-Broadway play.

Fifteen years and well over 20 film and television roles later, including a co-starring role in the film "Men Lie" Garry continues his career as an actor and playwright. He has worked with such stars as Robert DeNiro, Al Pacino, Jack Nicholson, Sly Stallone, Harrison Ford, and Bill Cosby, among others.

Now, at the beckoning of his nephew Todd, Garry has put together this insightful and humorous recipe book for college students— a recipe book that features wholesome and hearty meals and snacks that take an average of one half hour to prepare and are cost effective. After all, *"You're Not In Mom's Kitchen Anymore."*

Always an overachiever, Garry is currently working on a novel and a science fiction screenplay.

GINA LAGUARDIA

EDITOR

As editor-in-chief of *College Bound Magazine*, Gina LaGuardia masterfully re-tooled *You're Not In Mom's Kitchen Anymore!* to help Garry serve up some of the best, most scrumptious, and delectable recipes in the dorming world.

A 1994 graduate of the very cool, very hip New York University, with a younger brother just off to college, she's an expert on the ins-and-outs of surviving school. While growing up, her mom always cooked ooddles upon oodles of well-balanced, delicious meals, and her dad always lectured about the importance of "being independent." Needless to say, she knows the deal about dishin' it on your own.

Her "wordsmith" credentials include a college internship at *Redbook*, and an editorial assistantship with a food magazine right after graduation. After editing articles there about artichokes and apples, she worked for a time at *Woman's World Magazine* and kept up as a freelance writer for such savvy publications as *'TEEN Magazine*. It was through her freelance work for their fitness department that she discovered her true calling– writing for a teen readership. She has been very happy as the resident "teeny bopper lingo afficionado" at Ramholtz Publishing ever since.

Although she's not dorming any longer, she's still *not* in her mom's kitchen. In fact, she'll soon have to do some *pretty* impressive cooking when her fiance, Frank, becomes her hubby. And, boy is *he* glad she's got *Garry's Goods* to help back her up in the kitchen!

DEDICATION

I dedicate this book to my mother Karen. Although she is not with me, she is always here in spirit.

ACKNOWLEDGEMENTS

To my father Ralph, who always pushed me to do more and believes I can succeed at whatever I do.

To my sister Paula McCabe, for her recipes and advice.

To my brother Eric for always believing in me.

To my nephew Todd— without him I never would have written this book.

To Luciano Rammairone for having the faith and courage in this project from the start.

To Gina Biancardi for putting up with Luciano.

To Gina LaGuardia for toiling away the hours getting this book into shape.

To Giulio Rammairone and Suzanne Massaro for their creativity, unique sense of style, and artistic direction.

And, pats on the back from the friends who were excited about this project. It was their support that helped inspire me.

~ Garry Pastore

F O R E W A R D

So, you're getting ready to go off to college, or maybe you're already there. Well, have no fear– you *won't* be starving! Sure, cafeteria food is the pits sometimes, but when you really get the munchies for some home-cooked meals, *don't* go runnin' home– *do it yourself!* After all, college is a time of independence, on-your-own assertiveness, and most of all– *fun! "You're Not In Mom's Kitchen Anymore!"*

Read on for some of the hippest, funniest recipes you'll ever encounter! As you'll soon see, Garry is the best at dishin' to ya' the latest, greatest, and easiest recipes for munchies, soups, sauces, side dishes, salads, magnificent main courses, and delectable desserts. What's even better is that throughout the book, the whole college lifestyle is kept in mind. Each recipe has some helpful, fun icons that reveal those very important gotta-know-tidbits like serving size, time, cost, and gas probability factors.

If you need more information on
surviving other aspects of college life, we've got
those answers for ya', too! Be sure to point your
Web browser in the direction of **CollegeBound.NET**
at *http://www.cbnet.com*
We're the Best Bet On The Net For Teens!

In the meantime, wipe off that desk-countertop and get set to dorm-gourmet it up. Enjoy!

~ Gina LaGuardia,
Editor, *College Bound Magazine*

TABLE OF

CONTENTS

TOP *ten* LIST

10 I went to college so I know.

9 Going to college has you forever busy studying and partying– there's no time for any more complications. But hey– you gotta eat!

8 My nieces and nephews confirm this so don't even think about denying it.

7 Unlike Pre-Calc, Spanish II, and Physics, eating is not a requirement, it's a *necessity*.

6 Mommy is too far away!

5 Your "other half" probably doesn't know how to cook either– isn't it important that at least *one* of you knows which side of the stove is up?

4 Do you want to deal with all the technical mumbo-jumbo or just learn how to cook the darn thing?

3 Just think dudes: If you can cook up a good meal and play a love song on the guitar, she may very well fall head over heels in love with ya'!

2 Better yet, if you *can* cook for her and her parents when they come to visit, *while* playing a love song on the guitar, not only will *she* fall in love with you, but her folks probably will, too!

1 If school doesn't work out, you can always get a job as a line cook making $8 an hour.

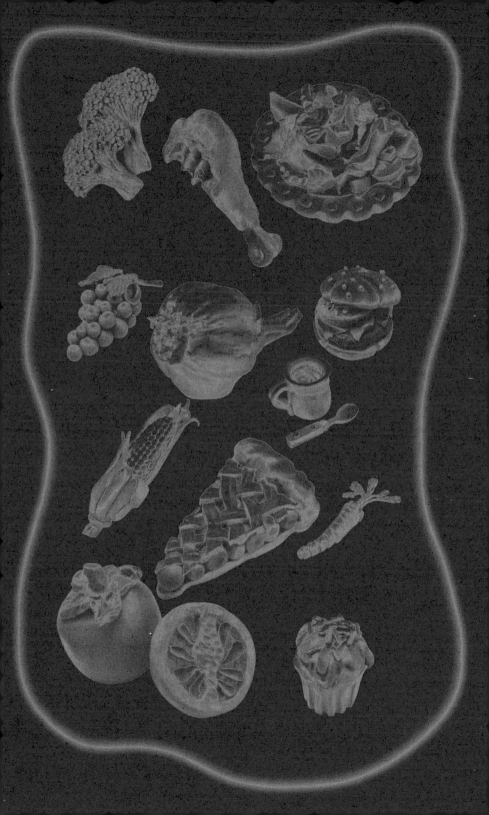

INTRODUCTION

I was sitting around one day talking to one of my nephews and my sis', and they were saying how cool it would be to come up with a cookbook for college students. My sis' has eight kids, and all of them go away to school so she knows what she's talking about. "They gotta eat, right!?"

When I went to college, I wasn't fortunate enough to have the luxury of attending a sleep-away school. However, I *did* move out of my house at an early age and had to fend for myself often without a clue— kinda' like you guys now! Of course, cooking was the biggest pain. I mean, when I was younger and still living at home— no matter where I was, I knew that if I got my butt to the table by 5 p.m., dinner would be waiting for me. That's why moms are so great. But, as you very well know by now, my "on-your-own friend," once you move out, it's a "dog eat dog world" out there.

So, all of a sudden I got this brain surge (rare for me, I'll have you know!). I decided to go to culinary school, figuring I could learn how to feed myself while getting an education.

Now *that's* thinking, right?! Anyway, back to the story— I'm not telling you that you must go to culinary school to be a good cook, but you should at least have the desire to learn *how* to cook— that's where I can help.

And don't despair, I've found that virtually *anyone* can cook if they have a fun teacher! My mom is a perfect example— she would put something on the stove and leave the room. Now I don't recommend this "trick" to you guys out there— my mom had a "gift." She would come back at any time— once one side of the slab of meat was nice and black, she would flip it over and blacken the other side. I remember watching some fat chef from New Orleans on TV making a big splash with his Cajun cooking and all this "blackened" stuff and I was like: "What's the big deal— my mom does that *all* the time!"

Anyway, without getting *too* complicated (you're in college, you have enough of that... I know!), I've tried to come up with a cookbook for you single schoolguys and gals where you won't have to shell out a lot of cash to eat well. For most of these fun-filled and yummy recipes, the cooking time is 30 minutes or less, and they're all quite pleasing to your pocket *and* your appetite!

As you'll see in the pages to follow, I've attempted to explain my gourmet galavantings in layman's terms— it's not that I am insinuating that all of you out there are *lame*— it's just that I know the deal with complex cuisine... you won't waste your precious time, right? Have no worries. I really don't have the time or the patience to read through some boring cookbook *either*, so I've done my best to entertain and enlighten you along the way. Have fun!

Cost Factor

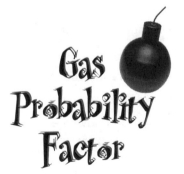

Gina's dad used to tell her that in looking forward to college, she should also look forward to "being broke." I'm sure you'll agree. There's books, pencils, lab fees, café latte with pals, and more— it's no wonder you barely have a nickel to spare! So, in keeping with this frugal functioning, if you feel that you don't have an abundance of funds from which to prepare your meals, you're wrong! With this book, I have given breakdowns of the approximate cost factor for each delectable dish. If you're cooking for a group, I will also list how many people get served— then you can all chip in.

Servings

How many of us get to eat "all for one or one for all"? Well, have no fear, here's some help! Check out this chit-chatterin' icon at the top of each recipe. It will equal the number of servings that the recipe releases. You may be able to do some cooking for a crowd or cut the recipe in half for a solo gourmet!

Gas Probability Factor

Picture this scenario: You've got this babe or dude you just met and you want to impress them with your cool culinary know-how. You invite him or her up to your dorm, whip up this great meal, and just as you're about to get romantic, your stomach starts to flip flop and emit obnoxious noises and noxious fumes. *Oh no!*

Time Factor

Time? Who has it? *(Not you!)* Who wants it? *(You– all the time!)* Who needs it? *(You, you, you!)* No, I *can't* give you more time, but I *can* cut down on the minutes and seconds you spend whipping up yummy, delicious food. Check my easy time factor icon to help you figure out those precious prep moments. And remember, if you have to prepare something and then let it sit, take advantage of the wait– study some flashcards, read a chapter of Chaucer, prepare for a speech! It'll make the time fly, and the assignments may even be done by dessert! Now, *that's* a perfect ending!

Fattening Factor

Of course we *can't* forget the fattening factor. That "Freshman Fifteen" may creep up on you if you don't watch out! So as not to have you *completely* food phobic throughout this entire book, I've only included the fattening factor in the dessert chapter– that's where it's the most lethal, anyway!

My gas probability factor will cut down *(no pun intended here!)* on such embarrassing mishaps. Hey– if you know ahead of time, you won't have anything to worry about.

Keep in mind that certain foods react on the digestive system differently, and affect certain people differently. If you see that an item you plan to prepare is gassy, substitute it. Here's a hint: If you're going to be a couple, gas could be a problem, but if there are several of you in one room, do what everybody else does– blame it on the other guy!

"Ovens, and toasters, and stoves, oh my!"

Face it, guys and gals– you'll need at least one of

the following utensils to get yourself a good meal.

Preferably a stove of some sort and an oven will do the trick.

Now I know that most dorms are small, but miniature versions of

these do not take up a lot of room. Check the sale circulars–

there are plenty of electric burners and hot plates to choose

from that are fairly cheap (and always on sale!).

THE PERFECT COLLEGE DORM SHOULD HAVE A:

- **two-burner electric stove**
- **toaster oven**
- **microwave**
- **small refrigerator**
- **blender**
- **hand mixer**

* This is a perfectly utensiled dorm– not every school allows all of this

equipment. Be sure to check with your dorm's officials for their

"utensil acceptability policy"! And remember: UNPLUG these

things when they're not in use, *especially* the electric stove!

UTENSILS

- A whisk is not to be used for anything other than whipping up sauces and dips.

- Your spatula is *not* a fly swatter. It is used to pick up food from hot frying pans and grills. (It's also great for speeding up grilled cheese sandwiches– smash them deeper toward the bottom of the pan to cook 'em up extra quick!)

- To extract sauces and soups from pots, use a ladle.

- A chef knife is not a weapon. Use it only for chopping garlic and onions– *not* to get back at a dormmate from hell!

- A cutting board is used to do that all-important garlic and onion chopping.

- Your frying pan is– you guessed it– used for frying. (It's *also* not to be used as a weapon.)

- Although it's tempting, try not to use your sauce pot as a hammer.

- A pasta pot should only be used accordingly– not as a catch basin for leaky roofs.

- Lastly, your pasta strainer should be used solely for removing water from pots– not for sifting sand at the beach!

- A measuring cup is extremely important. There's nothing worse than having not enough or too much stuff in your recipe.

HERBS & SPICES

There are several herbs and spices you should always have on hand to liven up the meal you plan to cook. To help you out, I'll list them in order of importance. By the way, most herbs and spices come in really cool spice racks, available at department and houseware stores all over. These "ready to go" racks save you time and money and are actually pretty cool-looking. If you land a really hip rack, consider it an investment in decor *and* delicacy!

SPICES
salt • black pepper • garlic powder • chili powder
onion powder • paprika • taco seasoning
cinnamon • nutmeg

HERBS
sage leaves • parsley flakes • basil flakes • Italian seasoning
pepper flakes • thyme flakes • rosemary leaves
poultry seasoning

STAPLE ITEMS

Staple items have nothing to do with holding your term paper pages together. In actuality (*ohhh - - big word!*), these are the items you absolutely must always have on hand. When the munchies come on (to be addressed in greater detail next), these staple items are must-haves in order to satisfy your hunger pangs! Here's my fave staple items, listed in order of importance...

CONDIMENTS
ketchup • mustard • *Hellman's®* mayonnaise • olive oil
vinegar • teriyaki sauce • *Worcestershire* sauce
hot sauce • taco sauce • *ReaLemon®* juice

REFRIGERATED
butter, margarine • milk • eggs • cheddar cheese
Monterey Jack cheese • grated Parmesan cheese
sour cream • flour tortillas • *Thomas' English Muffins®*
lettuce • tomatoes

DRY GOODS
pasta, spaghetti, ziti, etc. • *Uncle Ben's®* rice • taco shells
tortilla chips • *Lipton®* vegetable soup mix • all-purpose flour

CANNED GOODS
College Inn® chicken broth • *Del Monte®* tomato sauce
El Paso® sauce • sliced black olives
sliced jalapenos • canned tuna fish

PERISHABLES

Listed below are items that do not necessarily have a long shelf life in your refrigerator. If you know what's good for you (and don't want to get yourself dorm-evicted due to "stink-arama!"), prepare to do some same-day cooking. What's even more important than the odor is that you can get very sick from eating something that should have been eaten days before.

steak and all fresh beef • chopped meat • chicken • chicken cutlets • pork and pork products (unless smoked) • fresh fish •

*If the day comes that you want to have a clam bake, always remember: Lobsters, crabs, clams, and mussels must be both purchased and cooked while they are alive. (Kinda' gross, but great!)

If you *do* purchase something perishable and are not going to cook it right away, freeze it and defrost when needed.

REMEMBER THIS...

When reading the recipes from this book, please make sure you stick to the amount that I suggested in the recipe—I'm not writing these things just to read my own words!

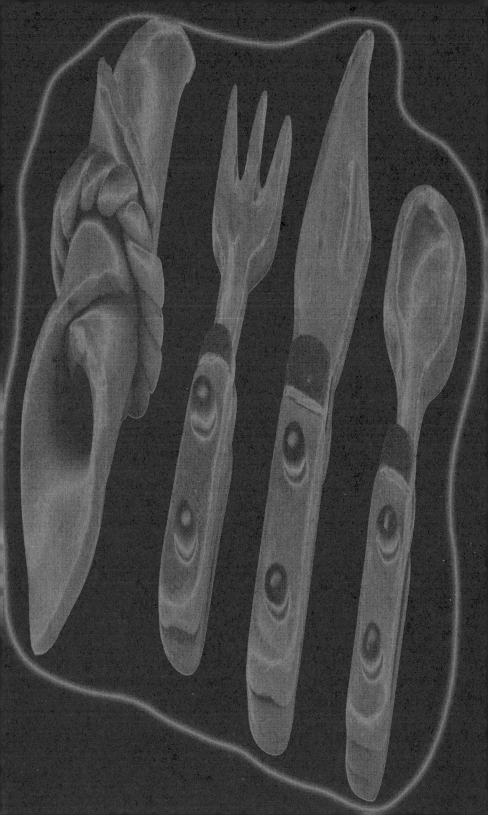

chapter
1

HIES

"Ya' gotta eat, right!?"

The "Munchies" is a weird phenomenon that occurs on college campuses at weird hours of the day and night. For some inexplicable reason, they most affect college students. FACT... Buffalo Wings were invented because of the munchie cravings. It's true— some dude was home for the holidays and got a case of the munchies, he then went to his father and told him. They rummaged around the kitchen, found some chicken wings, and proceeded to add butter, hot sauce and... presto! Buffalo Wings were born. Now I'm not saying that *all* experimentation works— that's the reason for this book in your very hands. Although experimentation can be fun, I prefer to satisfy my hunger right away rather than rummage around for something that might not work.

So, on that note, here's my own personal collection of some of the best munchie satisfying recipes I could find. And, they're *"GARRY GUARANTEED"* to work— get ready to feast away!

Bacon, Lettuce and Tomato Sandwich (B.L.T.)

Protein Alert–
A few slices of turkey are great on this sandwich, too! Find yourself with too much bacon? Don't worry, freeze it and save it for a weekend breakfast treat!

Sure, this one is kind of easy, but I don't want to scare you off right away! This will start you out slowly.

I N G R E D I E N T S

- 2-3 strips bacon
- 2 slices white bread
- 2 slices ripe tomato
- 3 pieces crispy lettuce
- *Hellman's®* mayonnaise

P R E P A R A T I O N

1) Pan fry or microwave bacon to your liking.
   (I prefer crispy.)
2) Remove and drain excess fat on paper towel.
3) Toast bread and add sliced tomato, lettuce, and bacon.
4) Smear with mayo and eat!

$2 per sandwich

0%

10 minutes

1 sandwich

Buffalo Wings

Back to the Buffalo! During study breaks, game celebrating, or plain ol' TV watchin', you can't go wrong with wings!

INGREDIENTS

- 25 chicken wings
- 1 cup *Durkee®* hot sauce
- ½ cup *Heinz®* Ketchup
- 1 stick butter
- ½ cup all-purpose flour
- ½ cup vegetable oil
- pinch of salt and pepper
- blue cheese dressing
- celery sticks (optional)

PREPARATION

1) Cut wings at joint.
2) Dump flour into a bowl; add salt and pepper to taste.
3) Heat oil in a frying pan.
4) While oil gets hot, *dredge* wings through the flour. When they all have a nice coating, add to hot oil carefully!
5) Brown wings on both sides and remove from heat; place them on paper towels to remove excess oil.
6) In a saucepot, melt butter; add hot sauce and ketchup, stir away with whisk.
7) When mixture is hot, give it a taste and add salt and pepper to your liking.
8) Add your wings, shimmy them up, then transfer to a dish.
9) Serve with celery sticks and blue cheese dressing. Munch on!

GARRY'S GOODS

Wanna' make a really awesome sandwich? Add your favorite luncheon meat (turkey, roast beef, or– ahhh, salami!) on top of melted cheese and cover with other half. You now have yourself one gnarly, garlicky sandwich!

75¢
per loaf

50%

20 minutes

4-5 cheesy chunks

Cheese 'n Garlic Bread

Easy, easy, easy! This is so easy to make and such a great munchie food. It's also great with a spaghetti and meatball dinner (pg. 70). Jazz it up with some cold cuts and you've got yourself one super-tasty sandwich.

INGREDIENTS

- 1 loaf Italian bread
- ¼ cup olive oil
- ½ stick butter
- ½ teaspoon garlic powder or 1 tablespoon fresh garlic, chopped
- ½ teaspoon parsley flakes
- ¼ cup parmesan cheese
- ¼ cup Monterey Jack cheese, chopped

PREPARATION

1) Preheat oven to 375°.
2) Cut Italian bread lengthwise; spread oil and butter on both sides.
3) Sprinkle garlic and cheeses down length of bread– don't be stingy! Dust with parsley.
4) Place bread on oven rack and bake at 300° for approximately 15-20 minutes or until golden brown.
5) Cut bread into cubes and eat!

Boss Burritos

Yeah, yeah, burritos are cool. And, they're also extremely easy to make. So, create away– you can stuff them with just about anything you want. My personal favorite is chopped meat, but depending on your taste, you can go for chicken, fish, or vegetables (if you're not a carnivore!).

INGREDIENTS

- 2 flour tortillas
- ¼ pound chopped meat
- ¼ cup onion, finely chopped
- 1 tablespoon *El Paso*® refried beans
- ¼ teaspoon chili powder
- 1 dash garlic powder
- ¼ teaspoon taco seasoning
- 1 tablespoon olive oil
- grated cheddar or Monterey Jack cheese
- lettuce, shredded
- tomato, chopped
- green pepper, chopped (optional)

PREPARATION

1) Put oil in frying pan and heat. When oil is hot, add chopped onion.
2) *Sauté* onion until translucent; add meat and watch it brown.
3) Next, add chili powder, garlic powder, and taco seasoning. Mix well with a wooden spoon and remove from heat.
4) Heat your tortilla on a grill or in the oven at 250° for five minutes. Do not brown tortilla! Those knuckleheads who do will only have brittle, cracked-up tortillas– no folding/stuffing potential there!
5) Place tortilla on counter and spread on refried beans; add meat and onion mixture in center. Sprinkle on the cheese and lettuce. Add tomato and pepper on top.
6) Fold tortilla from the bottom to form a pocket, then roll from the sides. Voila! Now you can eat it.

GARRY'S GOODS

You can even have these Boss Burritos for breakfast– just omit the chopped meat and refried beans and add scrambled eggs in their place.

GARRY'S GLOSSARY

to sauté:
When we say "sauté onions until translucent," it's really just fancy talk for cooking them up 'til they're clear and tender

75¢
per burrito

100%

20 minutes

2 burritos

GARRY'S GOODS

If the area you clean chicken on is not properly spic and span, this Italian guy named "Sal Monella" may pay ya' a visit and make you very sick! Take it from me— when working with chicken, always clean the area and the utensils you use with soapy water! There's nothing worse than Salmonella poisoning.

$5
for finger fun

50%

25 minutes

16 fingers

Chicken Fingers With Honey Mustard Dip

Chicken fingers and cramming for a test go hand in hand. Why, you ask? Simply because they're one of those glorious foods you don't have to eat with a knife and fork– in other words, your page-flipping hand is free!

INGREDIENTS

CHICKEN FINGERS -
- Package of *Purdue®* chicken tenders
- 1 cup vegetable oil
- 1 cup all-purpose flour
- 1 cup *4C Seasoned Breadcrumbs®*
- 2 whole eggs
- salt and pepper to taste

DIP -
- ½ cup *Gulden's®* mustard
- ¼ cup *Hellman's®* mayonnaise
- ¼ cup honey

PREPARATION

1) Heat oil in saucepan until very hot. Do not burn!
2) Wash tenders in water, drain; set aside.
3) In one bowl, put flour, salt, and pepper. Have another bowl for the breadcrumbs. In yet a third bowl, do some egg whipping with your whisk.
4) Dip the tenders in flour, then in egg, and finally in breadcrumbs. Make sure they are well-coated.
5) Carefully place tenders into the hot oil. They should begin to brown immediately.
6) Remove tenders from oil when golden brown and place on paper towels to drain.
7) In another bowl, whisk-mix your mustard, mayo, and honey. Transfer to a cup of some sort– your chicken fingers are ready for dipping.

Crudite With Vegetable Dip

Crudite is a really cool, non-fattening, palette-pleasing snack for those of you who are watching your weight. It's also a fun word to say, once you know how to! (See my *Goods*.) This veggie medley is also super-simple to prepare and is great to have at parties because it just sits there— you don't have to serve it.

I N G R E D I E N T S

VEGETABLES -
- 1-pound bag carrots
- 1-pound package celery
- 2-3 zucchini (medium size)
- 1 head cauliflower or broccoli (optional)

DIP -
- Package *Lipton®* Vegetable Soup mix
- 12-ounce container sour cream

P R E P A R A T I O N

1) Give vegetables a good rinse; peel skin from carrots; discard tops and root of celery.
2) Get ready to chop away! The idea is to cut the carrots, celery, and zucchini into two-inch-long strips about a 1/2-inch thick *(julienne)*. This makes them easy to pick up and dip.
3) If you want the broccoli and cauliflower, cut them below the flowers.
4) The dip is really easy to make: just empty contents of soup mix into a bowl, combine with sour cream, and whip with your whisk. Don't throw away sour cream container— you can use it to save the leftover dip.

GARRY'S GOODS

Pronunciation:
You say this:
Cru/dit/tay
as in—"Who the hay?"
not Crud/ite
as in— "You bite!"

GARRY'S GLOSSARY
julienne:
Strips cut ½-inch thick.

$4-5
per crudite crew

10%

25 minutes

34 Pals

GARRY'S GOODS

For something different, roll up a slice of American or cheddar cheese with the hot dog, then bake. Or, if you're throwing a party, roll the hot dogs as instructed, cut into bite-size pieces, and serve 'em up!

$4-5
for hot dog heaven

50%

20 minutes

5-6 people

Dogs In A Blanket

It's been said that dogs are a man's best friend. They've got that right! These hot dogs in a puff pastry are so simple to prepare and are always a real crowd pleaser!

I N G R E D I E N T S

- 1-pound package hot dogs
- 1 tube *Pillsbury®* Crescent Roll dough

P R E P A R A T I O N

1) The fun part is figuring out the *Pillsbury®* containers! Pop it against a counter and separate the dough; flatten it out as much as possible.
2) Put hot dog on the edge of dough and roll up.
3) Place on greased cookie sheet and bake at 350° until golden brown.

That's it!
Serve with Guldens' Spicy Brown Mustard®.

English Muffin Pizzas

By far, these pizzas are some of the best munchie foods ever created!

I N G R E D I E N T S

- 2 *Thomas' English Muffins*®
- ½ cup *Progresso*® pizza sauce or other leading brand
- 1 slice provolone cheese
- 1 tablespoon olive oil
- garlic salt and pepper to taste

P R E P A R A T I O N

1) Toast *Thomas' English Muffins*®; remove when slightly brown.
2) Sprinkle olive oil on muffins, spread sauce over oil, season with garlic and pepper, then top with cheese.
3) Put in toaster oven or regular oven at 325° for 5-7 minutes until cheese turns brown and bubbly.

GARRY'S GOODS

If you feel like getting crazy, you can add any one of your favorite toppings– sausage, mushrooms, pepperoni, whatever– before you bake it up!

per pizza

10%

10 minutes

2 pizzas

GARRY'S GOODS

Make sure that
the pot you
choose to use
is large enough
to hold three eggs and
cover them completely.

*Watching your weight?
Instead of using bread,
plop egg salad on top
of lettuce and go easy
on the mayo!*

$1-2
per sandwich

50%

20 minutes

2 sandwiches

Egg Salad Sandwich

Here's another eggstra-easy, quick, and nourishing hunger cure that also has great nutritional value. It's a little high in the cholesterol department so I wouldn't advise eating it everyday! FYI: This sandwich tastes best on a crispy roll or on toast of your choice.

INGREDIENTS

- 3 eggs
- ½ onion, finely minced
- 1 stalk celery, finely minced (optional)
- ½ cup *Hellman's®* mayonnaise
- salt and pepper to taste

PREPARATION

1) In a pot, add hot water, a pinch of salt, and boil. (See my *Goods!*)
2) When water begins to boil, carefully add eggs, being sure to avoid breaking their shells. Boil eggs for approximately 8-10 minutes and then remove from pot.
3) Let them cool for approximately one hour (they should be cold-cold!). If you're short on time (or patience), running them under cold water will speed up the process.
4) Peel your cool eggs completely and put them in a mixing bowl; add chopped onions and celery.
5) Mash eggs with fork until they are finely chopped. Add your mayo a little at a time and season with salt and pepper... done!

Egg 'n Cheese On a Roll

Why include another egg sandwich?
Because it's easy and nutritious.
It's also the perfect thing to have before class in
the morning or while you're studying in the dorm
at night– excellent with a tall glass of milk!

I N G R E D I E N T S

- 1 egg
- Your favorite bread or roll (best on a crispy Kaiser roll)
- 1 teaspoon butter or margarine or
  Pam® cooking spray
- 1 slice of your favorite cheese

P R E P A R A T I O N

1) Heat skillet; add teaspoon of butter (or spray Pam®
   evenly over pan), making sure pan is coated.
   Do not burn butter.
2) Crack egg. Without breaking the yolk, put it
   directly on your melted butter. This is called
   "Sunny Side Up." When the white of the egg starts
   to solidify, flip egg over so the yolk is touching the
   pan. This is called "Over Easy."
3) Once egg is flipped, lay your cheese on top and
   melt. Once it's melted, transfer to bread and eat!

$1
per egg "roll"

75%

7 minutes

1 sandwich

GARRY'S GOODS

If you have leftover fajitas, refrigerate them. When you're hit with another case of the munchies, wrap 'em in a wet paper towel and microwave on high for 30 seconds—they'll be as good as new!

$3-5
For Fajita Flavorin'

100%

15 minutes

2 Fajita pleasers

Fajitas

¡Hola muchachos y muchachas! Fajitas are similar to burritos, except you get more meat here than you would in a burrito. *Here's* the beef!

I N G R E D I E N T S

- 1 package chicken cutlets or strip steak
- 2 flour tortillas
- 1 onion, sliced
- 1 red pepper, sliced
- 1 yellow pepper, sliced
- 1 clove garlic, minced
- 1 tablespoon *El Paso®* refried beans
- ¼ teaspoon chili powder
- 1 tablespoon olive oil

P R E P A R A T I O N

1) Pan fry or grill chicken or steak.
2) In a frying pan, heat oil; when hot, add garlic and sliced onion, sauté until onions turn clear.
   Add peppers and chili powder, continue to sauté until tender.
3) Remove from heat.
4) Heat tortilla in oven at 250° for five minutes then spread on refried beans.
5) Slice chicken cutlet or steak into strips, add a few pieces to tortilla; top with onion and pepper mixture. Roll 'em up, plate it, and eat away!

Grilled Cheese

Believe it or not, it takes a certain amount
of talent to make a kickin' grilled cheese sandwich.
See, my mom could never get the cheese to
melt without making the bread black. Ah yes,
I remember now— that scrape-scrape sound and
that smell— yuck! The trick to avoiding this is
thinly sliced cheese and lots of patience.

I N G R E D I E N T S

- 2 pieces sliced bread— white, rye, whichever you like
- 2-3 slices of your favorite cheese
- 1 tablespoon butter, margarine, or *Pam*®
  cooking spray

P R E P A R A T I O N

1) Completely coat bottom of frying pan with either
   butter or *Pam*®. Heat on stove but do not let this burn.
   If it becomes brown, you have to start over again.
2) While your butter/*Pam*® is heating up (but not burning),
   make your GC sandwich outside of the pan.
3) Pop in your sandwich and let it sit for 1-2 minutes,
   then flip— make sure there is enough butter to coat
   each side of the bread.
4) If you think you need to "butter it up" some more,
   spread extra on ahead of time. Cover pan for
   remaining 1-2 minutes. This will melt your cheese.
5) When both sides are golden brown, remove your
   sandwich and eat!

GARRY'S GOODS

For an added treat,
add a few pieces
of sliced tomato
before you grill
your sandwich.
You can also smear
a small dab of
mayonnaise on both
sides of the bread
and grill for a unique
taste treat.

per cheese pleaser

4%

10 minutes

1 GC delight

GARRY'S GOODS

Having a party? Turn it into a fiesta! Make a few pizzas, cut into miniature pieces, and you'll have some really tasty, bite-sized hor d'oeurves.

$1
per pizza pizazz

75%

10 minutes

24 amigos

Mexican Pizza

Italian and Mexican combined– Mucho bene!

INGREDIENTS

- 2 flour tortillas
- $\frac{1}{4}$ cup *El Paso*® refried beans
- shredded cheddar, Monterey Jack cheese, or both
- $\frac{1}{4}$ cup jalapenos, sliced

PREPARATION

1) Preheat oven to 350°.
2) Place tortillas on top shelf and warm for about five minutes.
3) When heated, remove tortillas and spread on refried beans; cover with cheese and jalapenos.
4) Bake until cheese is melted.
5) Cut the pizza into eight slices just like you would a cake.

Nachos

Nachos are Beavis' and Butthead's™ favorite dish, and it's no surprise! Since it's as easy as pie to make, it'll probably be *your* fave, too.

I N G R E D I E N T S

- 1 large bag *Frito Lay®* tortilla chips
- 4-ounce can green chilies, chopped
- 1 bag cheddar cheese, shredded

P R E P A R A T I O N

1) In a small saucepan, melt cheese over very low heat, stirring constantly.
2) When cheese is partially melted, add chopped chilies.
3) Mix until completely melted and smooth.
4) Transfer to a bowl, grab your tortilla chips, and start your nacho dippin'.

GARRY'S GOODS

If you want, you can add some sliced peppers and lettuce and tomato to this cheesy treat.

$2
per sandwich

75%

15 minutes

1 sandwich

Philly Cheese Steaks

This is probably one of America's favorite sandwiches. I even admit to liking a big, juicy Philly Cheese Steak once in a while. In fact, this is my favorite tailgater treat at N.Y. Giants™ football games.

INGREDIENTS

- 3-4 pieces *Steak-Ums®* sandwich steaks
- 1 hoagie roll or ½ loaf Italian bread
- 1 whole onion, sliced
- 1 clove garlic, finely diced
- sliced cheddar cheese or Monterey Jack cheese
- 2 tablespoons oil

PREPARATION

1) Heat your frying pan, add oil.
2) When oil heats up, lay the steaks on top. They cook fast so be sure to cook one side and flip it over right away to cook up the other side.
3) Remove steaks from heat and keep warm.
4) Add chopped garlic and sliced onion to oil, sauté until onions turn clear.
5) Put meat on bread; add onions and cheese immediately so it melts itself. Cut in half and chow down, baby!

Potato Skins

"Gimme some skins!" These take a little time but are well worth the wait. They're great munchie food, and are also cool to serve at parties! The best part of all is that they're cheap, cheap, cheap!

INGREDIENTS

- 3 Idaho potatoes, unpeeled
- ½ cup cheddar cheese, shredded
- bacon bits

PREPARATION

1) Boil potatoes (unpeeled) in a small pot of hot water.
2) Do a forked potato tender test after 10 minutes. If it's tator-tender-pleasin', remove from heat, drain, and cool.
3) Cut potatoes in half lengthwise, then in half again.
4) Carefully scoop out some of the potato until you have about a quarter-inch of potato and skin.
5) Grease a cookie sheet with *Pam®* and place potato skins on greased sheet. Cover potato skins with cheese and bacon bits. Bake in oven or toaster oven at 250° until golden brown (about 20 minutes).

GARRY'S GOODS

What to do with leftover potato insides? Serve up a delectable breakfast the next morning by unwrapping the "tater-guts" you saved, adding some onions and pepper, and frying up— instant hash browns!

$2 per pack of skins

25%

25 minutes

12 skins

GARRY'S GOODS

You'll need at least two bags of tortilla chips for this— *(and a gas mask!)*

$12
per party bowl bundle

100%

25 minutes

20 people

Paula McCabe's Black Bean Dip

This *does* take a little time to make but it's great—especially if your college team is in the playoffs, you've all just passed your exams— *or* you've all just failed! Whatever the situation, this is a really happening party food.

INGREDIENTS

- 2 8-ounce cans of *El Paso®* refried beans
- 4-ounce can *El Paso®* chopped green chilies
- 1 envelope *El Paso®* taco seasoning mix
- 2 ripe avocados, cleaned and pitted
- 2 tablespoons ReaLemon®
- 1 small jar *El Paso®* taco sauce
- 1 pint sour cream
- 4-ounce can sliced black olives
- 6 ounces *Kraft®* cheddar cheese, shredded
- 1 tomato, chopped
- 1 onion, chopped

PREPARATION

1) Mix-whisk refried beans, green chilies, and taco seasoning mix.
2) Spread mixture on large round platter.
3) Blend the avocados (make sure you remove outer skin and pit), lemon juice, and taco sauce.
4) After this is blended, put on top of bean mixture.
5) Spread sour cream on top and sprinkle on olives, cheddar cheese, tomatoes, and onion.

Quiche

They say "Real men don't eat quiche." I say– "Bull..." I eat it and I never had anyone question me about my masculinity, so there! Here's an easy-as-pie basic quiche recipe, followed by a list of add-ins that you can quiche-customize to your liking. For those of you out there who don't have a clue as to what quiche is, it's basically an egg custard pie. Now, don't worry– I wouldn't even consider you making a pie shell from scratch, that's too much of a hassle. Don't fret– they sell great frozen crusts already made. Pick one up and let's begin.

I N G R E D I E N T S

- 8-inch frozen pie shell, thawed
- 3 whole eggs
- 2 cups half and half or heavy cream
- ½ teaspoon salt
- pinch of black pepper
- pinch of nutmeg
- 1-2 tablespoons of butter

P R E P A R A T I O N

1) Preheat oven to 375°.
2) Blend together eggs, cream, salt, pepper, nutmeg, and butter in a bowl. This will be your custard.
3) Prick bottom of pie shell with a fork. (Three pricks will do.) Add your filling, then top with your custard. Important: Leave at least a half an inch from top of pie to allow for rising.
4) Bake for 25-30 minutes or until quiche has puffed and browned.
5) Let cool slightly and cut in quarters.

Here's a few **Quiche-Customizin'** fillings. Don't be afraid to experiment– mushrooms, bacon, and Swiss cheese often make up a no-fail pie. Or, for you vegetarians out there– a tomato, zucchini, and onion mix are ideal. <u>OTHERS:</u> • *Bacon (Quiche Lorraine)* • *ham* • *turkey* • *swiss cheese* • *cheddar cheese* • *Monterey Jack cheese* • *sliced mushrooms* • *zucchini* • *broccoli* • *spinach* • *tomatoes* • *onions* • *red or yellow peppers* • *etc.*

21

GARRY'S GOODS

*A word to the wise...
Green peppers tend to
cause indigestion.
That's why I always
substitute yellow
for green peppers
whenever I can.
The yellow ones,
although a bit
more costly, are well
worth it in the long run.*

$3
per sausage supreme

75%

25 minutes

2 sandwiches

Sausage and Pepper Sandwich

This sandwich may not appeal to everyone out there, but I'm sure that if you're from one of the five boroughs of New York City, you must have had one of these tasty sandwiches at least once in your life. They're really popular at the famous annual "San Gennaro Feast" on Mulberry Street in Little Italy.

INGREDIENTS

- 3 Italian sausage links (sweet or hot)
- 2 bell peppers (red, yellow, or green), sliced into strips
- ½ onion, sliced
- 1 clove garlic, minced
- ¼ cup olive oil
- 2 hoagies, hero rolls, or 1 loaf Italian bread

PREPARATION

1) You can either grill, broil, or sauté your sausage. It is very important to cook it thoroughly–medium rare just won't do! Be sure to cook 'em up at least 15-20 minutes.
2) After sausages are cooked, put oil in the frying pan and heat. Add garlic and onion.
3) When onion turns clear, add pepper strips; sauté until tender.
4) Transfer sausage to the bread, slice down the middle, add pepper and onion mixture to the sausage, and that's it!

Rockin' Roast Beef Sandwich

Here's a quick and easy sandwich. All you'll need is some freshly sliced roast beef from your local deli. This super sandwich is best on a crispy roll. The absolute greatest part about it is that you can warm it up in the microwave.

INGREDIENTS

- ¼ pound roast beef, freshly sliced
- ¼ cup *Open Pit®* barbecue sauce
- 1 crispy Kaiser or hero roll

PREPARATION

1) Place roast beef in a microwave safe dish; pour BBQ sauce on top, and set it in microwave on high for 60 seconds.
2) Transfer to roll, grab a napkin, and munch away!

That's it–
You can break the land speed record for sandwich-making on this one!

GARRY'S GOODS

You don't always have to use roast beef for this— leftover steak or prime rib from last night's dinner work equally well.

$2.50 per sandwich

25%

5 minutes

1 sandwich

$1 50
per serving

75%

15 minutes

2 tacos

Tacōs

Ah yes, mis amigo– tacos are what make *Taco Bell*® so famous! I don't know what it is about Mexican food that's so attractive. I mean, it's very gassy and always gives you heartburn, but it still stands to be about the most popular type of food with college kids in America.
So, on that Mexican tip, here's a recipe for some easy-to-throw-together tacos that fill the munchie void.

I N G R E D I E N T S

- 2 *El Paso*® taco shells
- ½ cup ground beef
- ¼ onion, chopped
- ¼ cup vegetable oil
- ¼ cup *El Paso*® taco sauce
- ¼ cup taco seasoning
- pinch of garlic powder
- pinch of chili powder

TOPPINGS
- ¼ cup lettuce, shredded
- 1 tomato, chopped (optional)
- ¼ cup cheddar cheese, grated (optional)

P R E P A R A T I O N

1) Sauté onion in vegetable oil; when it turns clear, add ground beef and sauté.
2) When through, drain off excess fat. Add taco seasoning, garlic powder, and chili powder to meat and onions; mix well.
3) Remove mixture from heat and fill shell. Spoon taco sauce over meat mixture, cover with lettuce, tomatoes, and most importantly– cheese!

Tuna Salad

Indeed, tuna salad is not for everyone, however, it is very versatile and easy to make. And, if you make it the right way, it's not fattening, and it contains lots of protein for those "toner-uppers" looking to maximize their muscle mass.

I N G R E D I E N T S

- 1 can *Bumble Bee*® chunk white tuna in water
- 2 pieces sliced white bread
- 2 tablespoons *Hellman's*® mayonnaise
- pinch of salt and pepper
- 1 stalk celery, finely chopped (optional)
- ½ small onion, finely chopped (optional)

P R E P A R A T I O N

1) Drain water out of tuna can, dump into a small bowl, and mash it up with a fork.
2) Take sliced bread, remove the crusts, dice 'em up, and add to tuna– these edges act as a binder to the tuna– in other words, they hold it together.
3) Add your mayonnaise, salt and pepper, and mix together well.
4) If you're into the celery and onion deal, toss them in and mix away.
5) Dab on some white or rye bread, gob it on a roll, or serve up a healthy tuna heaping on a nice bed of lettuce.

S O U

chapter
2

P S

Soup is probably one of my *favorite* things to make and eat. Even though both *Campbell's*® and *Progresso*® make wonderful soups, and there is nothing easier than opening up a can and heating it on the stove, when it comes down to it– homemade soup takes the cake!

Most of my recipes call for the use of canned broth or bouillon cubes– these'll have them tasting "almost homemade."

Soup is really great on those cold, wet and rainy days– you've gotta' agree that there isn't anything more satisfying. The hottest part is that most of these are easy to make ahead of time and then warm up later.

SOME "SUPER SOUP" KNOWLEDGE: All soups contain a mixture of finely diced vegetables that include carrots, celery, and onions. This is known as a *mirepoix,* pronounced: *mir/or/pwa.*

Also, keep in mind that your soup should be allowed to simmer for at least one half hour. Oh, and one more secret– they usually taste better the next day.

GARRY'S GOODS

There are enough vitamins and nutrients in here to make your momma proud. For those with big appetites, have no fear. You can even eat this as a meal— barley is surprisingly very filling!

Always have everything you need to make your recipe handy— or as the French say it (and as I will repeat time and time again)— "Mise en Place", meaning: "everything in its place."

$3
per quart

75%

35 minutes

2 quarts

Beef and Mushroom Barley

Here's a handy dandy soup to have when you're freezin' your butt off. If you're really lucky, you can use some leftover steak in the fridge. If you don't have any, a cheap chuck steak will do. If you're a vegetarian, omit the beef altogether.

I N G R E D I E N T S

- 1 cup ½-inch beef cubes, cooked
- 1 package barley
- 1 cup mushrooms, sliced
- 1 carrot, peeled and finely diced
- 1 stalk of celery, finely diced
- 1 medium onion, finely diced

- 3 pinches fresh parsley, finely chopped
- ¼ cup vegetable oil
- 2 cans *College Inn®* beef broth
- ¼ cup cooking sherry wine
- pinch of thyme
- pinch of salt and pepper

P R E P A R A T I O N

1) Have your *mise en place* ready (See my *Goods*)
2) After rinsing barley, drain with colander; place in small saucepan.
3) Cover barley with about one quart of tap water; boil for 30-45 minutes.
4) When barley is tender, drain it one more time and then give it a final rinse. (It's a good idea to do this ahead of time to save valuable prep minutes.)
5) Heat oil in a large saucepan and add your *mirepoix* (celery, carrots, onion).
6) When onions start to clarify, add sliced mushrooms and sauté.
7) Add beef and barley, stir well.
8) Add your beef broth (minus the cans— ha ha, that's a joke!). Throw in the sherry, thyme, parsley, salt and pepper.
9) Let your concoction simmer for at least 30 minutes— then she's done.

Beef Vegetable

This is almost the same preparation as my filling Beef Barley soup except this time, you're adding vegetables and omitting the barley. You may also leave your carrots, celery, and onions chunky. Most importantly, this is a satisfying hearty soup to suit even the pickiest eater. If you want to have it vegetarian style, omit the beef and just use a vegetable stock instead of beef broth.

I N G R E D I E N T S

- 1 cup ½-inch beef cubes, raw
- 2 cans *College Inn*® beef broth
- 1 carrot, peeled and sliced
- 1 stalk celery, sliced into ¼-inch pieces
- 1 small onion, cubed into ¼-inch pieces
- 1 cup mushrooms, quartered
- 1 yellow squash, cubed
- 1 green zucchini, cubed
- 1 large tomato, cubed
- 1 baking potato, peeled and cubed
- ¼ cup vegetable oil
- ¼ cup cooking sherry wine
- pinch of thyme
- 3 sprigs fresh parsley, chopped or 3 tablespoons parsley flakes
- pinch of salt and pepper

P R E P A R A T I O N

1) Heat oil in large saucepan; add chopped onion, carrots, and celery; sauté.
2) Add beef, zucchini, squash, mushrooms, and potato. Continually stir with wooden spoon so your vegetables don't burn.
3) Add beef broth and sherry; throw in herbs and spices.
4) Add chopped tomato last– this keeps it from breaking apart.
5) Let soup simmer for at least 30 minutes or until carrots and potatoes are fork tender. Eat some now then save some for later!

GARRY'S GOODS

Dark meat (thighs and legs) are tastier for this soup, but white meat (breast meat) works equally well.

HEALTH TIP:
If you want a soup lower in calories and fat, remove the chicken skin before making your soup.

$2⁵⁰

per 2 bowls

50%

1 hour

2 quarts

Chicken Soup

A.K.A. Jewish Penicillin

If there is any one thing that I looked forward to when I was illin', it was my mom's chicken soup. She wasn't Jewish, and you don't have to be to make it. As most of us know, however, legend has that it's supposed to be a cure-all. I don't care what you say— there's no canned product out there that's as good as homemade chicken soup. The real way to make it is to buy a chicken and boil it with a *mirepoix* for hours. But since we *are* on a time schedule here, we'll cheat a little bit. The produce section of your local grocery should sell soup greens— all the stuff you want comes ready to go in those handy dandy little packages. Ya' see... you learn something new everyday!

INGREDIENTS

- 2-4 pieces of fresh chicken parts, (preferably thighs)
- 2 cans *College Inn*® chicken broth
- 1 large carrot, peeled and finely diced
- 2 stalks celery, washed and finely diced
- 1 medium onion, finely diced
- ¼ cup vegetable oil
- ¼ cup cooking sherry
- ¼ cup fresh parsley
- ¼ cup fresh dill or parsley
- 1 bay leaf

PREPARATION

1) Put oil in large saucepan, sauté mirepoix.
2) When onions clarify, add chicken and cook slightly for five minutes on both sides.
3) Add chicken broth, sherry, and herbs; simmer for 30 minutes or until chicken is cooked. To figure this out, prick with a fork until juices run clear.
4) Remove chicken pieces from soup, let cool for 10 minutes in the fridge or a half hour at room temperature.
5) When cooled, pull chicken apart with your fingers— if you like your soup chunky, put chicken in as is, if not, dice it up with a knife.

Pasta Fagioli

Italian for Pasta with Beans

This is my favorite soup in the whole wide world. When I was growing up, my Italian father would whip up what they called "peasant soups" like the ones he ate as a child. The soups were labeled as such because they fed a whole family and were reasonable to make when it came down to dollars and cents. In those days they didn't have a lot of money (kind of like your situation now!), so they tried to make a little go a long way. (Sound familiar?!)

INGREDIENTS

- 2 cloves garlic, finely chopped
- 1 medium onion, finely chopped
- 2-3 pieces bacon or prosciutto, finely chopped
- ¼ cup olive oil
- 1 large can of *Progresso®* white cannelli beans
- 1 large fresh tomato, seeded and cubed
- 2 cans *College Inn®* chicken broth
- 1 cup dry macaroni
  (preferably small shells, elbows, or dittalini, etc.)
- ¼ cup fresh Italian parsley, chopped
- pinch of salt and pepper
- ¼ cup grated parmesan cheese (garnish)

PREPARATION

1) Heat olive oil in medium saucepan, add chopped bacon, stir; do not make bacon crisp.
2) Add garlic and onion to the bacon and sauté until onion turns clear.
3) Add your tomato and beans, then in goes your chicken broth and parsley.
4) When soup starts to boil, add pasta and *simmer.*
5) When pasta is done, so is the soup. Pour into your favorite bowl and sprinkle with cheese— "Mmm, mmm, good!"

$2⁵⁰

lotsa pasta fagioli

75%

25 minutes

2 quarts

GARRY'S GOODS

For this one, the Nissin brand of *"Oodles of Noodles®"*, which come in a variety of flavors, is the best!

$1
per bowl

10%

10 minutes

1 bowl

Ramen

More affectionately known as Oriental Noodle Soup, this stuff should really be a staple item in everyone's kitchen cabinet. I recently bought five packages for a dollar– can ya' beat that bargain!? The great thing about these soups is that they're done in about 3-5 minutes and you can add all kinds of things to enhance their flavor. I will list some possibilities that make for super soup– choose one, or put all of them in, it's entirely up to you. Whatever you choose, cook it ahead of time so you can just chuck it in and chomp away!

POTENTIAL ADD-INS

- egg
- snow peas
- roast pork, sliced
- string beans
- sliced chicken breast
- parsley
- broccoli florets
- shrimp
- spinach
- stir-fry vegetables
- julienne carrots
- mushrooms
- julienne celery
- zucchini squash
- julienne bell pepper
- tomatoes

PREPARATION

1) Boil two cups of water. Add noodles and one or all of the ingredients listed above.
2) Stir in *Ramen* seasoning package and cook for three minutes over a low to medium flame. Remove from heat– get down, baby and eat!

CREAM SOUPS

"Proceed with diet caution but delicacy delight!"

Cream soups are great, but there is a little more preparation involved than with regular soups. You will also need a blender or food processor. *Braun®* makes something called a hand wand, or hand mixer. It costs about $20 and I always use it. In fact, I recommend you get one— it's easy to use, clean, and store, and it's very practical.

Because we often use butter and cream in their preparation, cream soups can be fattening, so those who are ultra-weight conscious should watch their intake.

Lastly, when making cream soups, we need to incorporate a thickening agent called a <u>roux</u> (pronounced: ROO, like "Boo!"), which is made up of butter and flour.

Be sure to follow my instructions completely because I want your soup to come out just the way I like it... excellent!

GARRY'S GOODS

Just In Case You Forget..
A _mirepoix_ is a mixture of finely diced vegetables that include carrots, celery, and onions.

$4
a quart

100%

30 minutes

2 quarts

Cream of Broccoli

Cream of broccoli is great— if you like broccoli. If you don't, I suggest you turn the page!

INGREDIENTS

- 1 package frozen or one head of fresh broccoli
- 2 cans *College Inn®* chicken broth
- 1 pint heavy cream
- ¼ cup cooking sherry
- 1 carrot, peeled and finely diced
- 1 stalk celery, finely diced
- 1 onion, finely diced
- 1 stick butter
- ¼ cup all-purpose flour
- ¼ cup fresh parsley, chopped
- pinch of salt and pepper

PREPARATION

1) Boil broccoli until tender (about 10 minutes); strain and cool. Next, if the broccoli is not already chopped, chop away.
2) When chopped, save some for garnish (¼ cup will do); set aside.
3) In a large saucepan, melt butter over a medium flame— be careful not to burn it.
4) When butter melts, add mirepoix; when onion clarifies, add broccoli and sauté.
5) Add flour a little at a time, stirring constantly with a wooden spoon until you have this green globby paste on the bottom (this is the infamous *roux*).
6) Cook this flour mixture for at least five minutes until the pasty flour taste is gone.
7) Add sherry, stirring continually with wooden spoon.
8) Add heavy cream and chicken broth. The paste should now start to resemble a cream soup— do you recognize it yet?
9) Now it's time to throw in the chopped parsley, salt and pepper. Let this all simmer for 20-25 minutes on a low flame.
10) When soup is done, blend with your wand (throwing in an "Abracadabra" is optional here!), or transfer to a food processor and blend until creamy.
11) Remove from processor, garnish with broccoli you saved, and season to taste if needed.

Cream of Carrot

"What's up, doc?" This soup is great if you like carrots. Plus, for this one you don't need to make a *roux*– the carrots will act as the thickening agent here. A word of friendly advice: You must realize that not every recipe in this book will appeal to everyone. If you know you like carrots, take a shot at this soup. If you don't, no need to experiment– I won't be insulted!

I N G R E D I E N T S

- 1 bag carrots, peeled and diced
- 2 stalks celery, cleaned and diced
- 1 medium onion, diced
- 1 stick butter
- 2 cans *College Inn®* chicken broth
- 1 pint heavy cream
- ¼ cup parsley, freshly chopped
- pinch of nutmeg
- pinch of salt and pepper

P R E P A R A T I O N

1) Boil carrots until tender (about 20 minutes).
2) While carrots are boiling, start to sauté onion and celery in butter in another saucepan. When they soften, set aside.
3) Drain carrots and cool with cold water; put celery and onion back on flame and add carrots.
4) Stir in cream and chicken broth, add nutmeg, salt and pepper.
5) Simmer on a low flame for 20 minutes; remove and puree in a blender. Garnish with chopped parsley.

Give it the greens! Don't forget to garnish with the parsley, that's what it's for.

$3
per quart

0%

25-30 minutes

2 quarts

Cream of Celery

Here's another very flavorful soup that needs a *roux*. Keep in mind that this one must be strained after puréeing to remove the veiny·fibers that run through the stalks of celery. Ya' gotta get rid of those suckers!

For those not into cooking lingo, a bunch of celery equals a handful.

I N G R E D I E N T S

- 1 bunch celery, cleaned and finely chopped
- 1 carrot, peeled and finely diced
- 1 large onion, finely diced
- 1½ sticks of butter
- ¼ cup all-purpose flour
- 2 cans *College Inn®* chicken broth
- 1 pint cream
- ¼ cup cooking sherry
- pinch of salt and pepper
- ¼ cup fresh parsley, chopped (garnish)

P R E P A R A T I O N

1) In a large saucepan, melt butter and add onion.
2) Throw in celery and carrots, stirring constantly with wooden spoon.
3) When celery starts to wilt (poor guys!), add the flour a little at a time, also stirring frequently; do this for at least 5-10 minutes or until the flour starts to brown.
4) Add your sherry, scraping all bits of flour from the side of pot.
5) Add the cream and chicken broth, salt and pepper; simmer for 20 minutes.
6) Remove from heat and purée. Strain through a kitchen sieve and garnish with chopped parsley.

$2⁵⁰

per quart

0%

27 minutes

2 quarts

Cream of Chicken

*For a hot soup, this one's pretty cool–
perfect for a cold winter day.*

INGREDIENTS

- 2-3 pieces fresh chicken, minus the skin
  (use at least one piece of breast meat)
- 2 cans *College Inn®* chicken broth
- 1 cup cold tap water
- ¼ cooking sherry
- 1 pint heavy cream
- 1 large carrot, peeled and finely diced
- 2 stalks celery, finely diced
- 1 onion, peeled and finely diced
- 1 stick butter
- ¼ cup flour
- ¼ cup fresh, chopped parsley
- pinch of salt and pepper

PREPARATION

1) In a medium saucepan, boil together chicken broth, tap water, and chicken pieces on medium flame until chicken is cooked (about 10 minutes).
2) Remove chicken from liquid but do not discard liquid (this is the stock). Let chicken cool to the point where it doesn't burn your hands. (You can speed this cooling process up by running the chicken under tap water.)
3) Remove all meat and chop finely, this will only be used as your garnish.
4) Melt butter in large saucepan– be sure not to burn it. Add your mirepoix and sauté.
5) When celery becomes soft, add flour a little at a time, stirring constantly with wooden spoon.
6) After about five minutes, add cooking sherry and heavy cream; continue stirring.
7) Add liquid stock (saved from before) a little at a time, continually stirring; reduce flame and simmer for 20 minutes.
8) Remove from heat and purée (blend) until smooth and velvety. Add your chicken pieces, chopped parsley, salt and pepper. Enjoy!

GARRY'S GOODS

To make this soup even heartier, add some vegetables or rice.

per quart

25%

25 minutes

2 quarts

$3
per quart

0%

25 minutes

2 quarts

Cream of Mushroom

Cream of Mushroom is my personal favorite, but unfortunately, mushrooms do not appeal to everyone. If you are a mushroom connoisseur as I am, there are many varieties available, but remember– the fancier the mushroom, the costlier.

INGREDIENTS

- 1 package button mushrooms
- 1 small onion, finely diced
- 1½ sticks butter
- ¼ cup flour
- ¼ cup cooking sherry
- 2 cans *College Inn®* chicken broth
- 1 pint heavy cream
- pinch of salt and pepper
- ¼ cup parsley (garnish)

PREPARATION

1) Rinse mushrooms and remove stems, placing them in a separate bowl. Set aside for later use. Do not throw away stems!
2) Slice mushrooms in half, then in half again (this is called quartering); set aside.
3) Melt one stick of butter in large saucepan (save the other half).
4) Add onions to butter and sauté until clear; add mushroom stems and sauté again. When these become soft, add flour a little at a time. This will become your "roux."
5) Stir roux with wooden spoon for at least five minutes.
6) Add sherry, continue stirring; add cream and chicken broth, simmer for 15 minutes.
7) Get your sieve and strain soup into another pot, pushing as much of the pulp through as you can. When through, set aside.
8) In a separate sauté pan (frying pan), melt the remaining half stick of butter; add remaining mushrooms and give them a quick sauté until they soften.
9) Add sautéed mushrooms to the strained soup mixture, and voila: Mushroom Soup!

Cream of Vegetable

Here's your basic vegetable soup with a creamy consistency. We will use a chicken base for this, and feel free to omit certain items. If there is a vegetable listed below that you don't care for or even one you would like to add, be my guest. After all, it *is* your soup!

GARRY'S GOODS

Make up some Cheese 'n Garlic Bread (pg. 5) with this one!

INGREDIENTS

- 1 large onion, diced
- 2 stalks celery, cleaned and diced
- 2 carrots, peeled and diced
- 1/4 cup parsley, chopped
- 1 yellow squash, diced
- 1 medium zucchini squash, diced
- 1-2 baking potatoes, peeled, boiled, and diced
- 1 stick butter
- 2 cans *College Inn®* chicken broth
- 1 pint cream
- 1/4 cup cooking sherry
- pinch of nutmeg
- pinch of salt and pepper

PREPARATION

1) Melt butter in a large saucepan; add mirepoix and sauté until onions clarify.
2) Add squash, potatoes, and parsley, stirring constantly with a wooden spoon.
3) Add cooking sherry, cream, and chicken broth.
4) Simmer for 20-25 minutes on low flame.
5) When carrots and potatoes are tender, remove from heat; add nutmeg and salt and pepper.
6) Blend or puree soup and serve.

$3.50 per quart

50%

25 minutes

2 quarts

GARRY'S GOODS

You can often find leeks in your supermarket; they resemble a large scallion. (If you don't know what a scallion is, too bad– I'm not explaining!) Anyway, if you can find them, pick 'em up– they will definitely enhance your soup's flavor.

Super Soup–
A spoon of sour cream goes nicely on top of this one.

$2⁵⁰

per quart

10%

30 minutes

2 quarts

Cream of Potato

This is another one of those warm-up-your-cold-bones kind of soups, and there are several varieties of it. Potato and Leek are very popular. Just for your info, a leek is a vegetable– *not* what guys exclaim they have to do after drinking beer! *A tip:* Since leeks tend to be sandy, use the lower portion of them only. Cut off the root and top portion, leaving the white bottom. Cut that in half and wash well to remove all the dirt.

INGREDIENTS

- 4-5 Idaho baking potatoes, peeled, washed, and cubed
- 1 onion, peeled and finely chopped
- 1 stick butter
- 1 leek, cleaned well and finely chopped (optional)
- 1 stalk celery, finely chopped
- 1 small carrot, peeled and finely chopped
- 2 cans *College Inn®* chicken broth
- 1 pint heavy cream
- ¼ cup cooking sherry
- pinch of salt and pepper
- ¼ cup fresh parsley (garnish)

PREPARATION

1) Boil potatoes in a medium saucepan until they are fork tender, about 20 minutes.
2) Remove from heat, strain, and cool.
3) Melt butter in a separate pan; sauté onion, carrot, celery, and the optional leek.
4) Add potatoes and cooking sherry; mix well.
5) At this point, the potatoes should start to soften and resemble mashed potatoes. Add the chicken broth and heavy cream.
6) Keep mixing– this soup should simmer on a very low flame because it has a tendency to burn. (If it does, the only thing to do is dump it!)
7) Simmer this way for 15 to 20 minutes.
8) Remove from heat and blend; finish it off with a quick garnish of parsley.

Cream of Zucchini

Gad Zukes! Just when you thought it was over,
I pulled another vegetable out of my hat!
Actually my sister turned me on to this soup and
it is outrageous. No mirepoix or roux are needed!

GARRY'S GOODS

This soup is great
either hot or cold.
For an added treat,
glob some sour
cream on top.

INGREDIENTS

- 3-4 medium zucchini
- 1 medium onion
- 2 cans *College Inn®* chicken broth
- ¼ stick of butter
- 1 pint heavy cream

PREPARATION

1) Wash and peel zucchini– to be called "zukes" from
   now on in!
2) Slice zukes into thin coins.
3) Peel and slice onion.
4) Melt butter in sauce pan, do not burn!
5) Add onion and sauté until clear. Add zukes and
   continue sautéing.
6) When zukes are tender, add broth and cream.
7) Simmer on low flame for 10 minutes.
8) Remove from heat. Blend or whip with hand wand.

$3.00
per quart

50%

15 minutes

1 quart

SAU

chapter 3

CES

Just think what food would be like if we didn't have sauces to put on them. Imagine pasta without tomato sauce? Or meatloaf and mashed potatoes without brown sauce? Ugh... dry, bland, boring!

They sell canned and bottled sauces, just like the soups, but I have to admit, although I "can" deal with canned soup, canned sauces are out of the question. To tell you the truth, since we already learned how to make a roux, we're halfway sauced up! That's basically all you really need to make a sauce— a roux, a stock (broth), and that's it!

To follow are several different sauces for you to make for both pasta and meat dishes. These are the most basic of sauces you will learn to prepare— I call them the "MOTHER SAUCES."

Once you've gotten the hang of it, get creative— from the sauce recipes I've given you, other sauces can be created. When I went to culinary school some 15 years ago, these were the first sauces I learned to make; it was from these very recipes that I've made probably over two hundred others since then!

By the way, sauces do not really produce any gaseous problems, so I have removed the gas probability factor from this chapter. It will gladly return later. *(Sorry!)*

GARRY'S GOODS

I will list recipes in the next chapter for use of this sauce. Also, adding sautéed mushrooms, peas, and chopped ham to this sauce makes it extra special.

You have to serve and eat this one right away or else it turns to concrete.

$3
per pint

15 minutes

3-4 servings

Alfredo Sauce

This sauce I'm sure you have heard of— does "Fettuccine Alfredo" ring a bell? It's made from cream and parmesan cheese, is easy to make, but is very fattening, heavy, and high in the cholesterol department. This sauce is best served over fettuccine noodles. Linguine or spaghetti will do just as well!

INGREDIENTS

- 1 box *Ronzoni®* fettuccine
- 1 pint heavy cream
- ½ stick butter
- 1 egg
- ½ cup good quality fresh romano or parmesan cheese (Locatelli romano is the best!)
- ¼ cup fresh parsley
- pinch of nutmeg
- pinch of salt and pepper

PREPARATION

1) In a large pot, boil water for fettuccine or other pasta. When water comes to a rolling boil— in other words, when large bubbles start poppin' up— it's ready! Add pasta and stir constantly (this keeps the pasta from sticking together).
2) In a medium saucepan, melt butter; add heavy cream and bring to a boil. Once it's there, turn down heat and simmer.
3) In a small mixing bowl, separate egg yolk from egg white. To do this, wash your hands well and let the white of the egg slide through your fingers.
4) Throw away egg white and add a small amount of hot cream mixture to yolk; whip well. Take a little more of the cream mixture and do the same until they are about the same temperature.
5) Once you have your egg mixture at the same temperature as the cream mixture on the stove, remove it from heat and combine with egg mixture.
6) Add half of the necessary cheese and whisk. Strain pasta, and transfer back to the pot.
7) Pour Alfredo Sauce over pasta and mix well. Add remaining cheese, chopped parsley, and seasoning.

Brown Sauce

This sauce is good on everything from meatloaf to roast beef, and it lasts for a good while in the fridge. This is great because it's one of those yummy things you can make way ahead of time and then freeze for future feasting. For this sauce, you'll need to find an item called *Gravy Master®*. Although it isn't essential, it does help to make a nice and hearty brown gravy.

You'll want to cook this roux a little longer— the darker it gets, the better. Tip: Adding sliced mushrooms can give it a little more zip!

I N G R E D I E N T S

- 1 can *College Inn®* beef broth
- ¼ cup flour
- ½ stick butter
- ¼ cup cooking sherry
- 1 tablespoon *Gravy Master®*
- pinch of thyme
- pinch of salt and pepper

P R E P A R A T I O N

1) Melt butter in a medium saucepan; add flour to make roux. Stir constantly with a wooden spoon.
2) When roux is an amber color, add cooking sherry and continue to stir; add beef broth a little at a time until sauce thickens.
3) Add seasonings and *Gravy Master*. Let sauce cook on medium heat for about 20 minutes, stirring occasionally. Try not to stir up from bottom because sometimes the bottom will burn and ruin the sauce.
4) Strain through sieve; either save it or serve it.

per pint

15 minutes

1 quart

GARRY'S GOODS

For macaroni and cheese casserole, boil elbow macaroni until tender (about 10 minutes). Strain the macs and then pour cheese sauce over it; mix well and put in casserole dish. Bake at 350° for about 20-25 minutes, until top gets brown and crusty.

$3

per pint

15 minutes

1 pint

Cheese Sauce

Cheese sauce is great on vegetables, especially over broccoli or cauliflower. And, how can we forget the ever popular macaroni and cheese?! You can even use this recipe for a fondue— if a fondue suits you! Even though this sauce is a "cheese to please", it's not meant to keep very long— it should be eaten right away. The recipe shown here is made with cheddar cheese, but you can use any kind you like. I like cheddar because of its melting quality. Some other cheeses, like Swiss, become elastic and do not melt well— watch out for clumps!

INGREDIENTS

- 1 cup sharp cheddar cheese, shredded
- 1 pint heavy cream
- ½ stick butter
- ¼ cup flour
- pinch of salt and pepper

PREPARATION

1) Melt butter in medium saucepan; add flour and stir constantly with wooden spoon.
2) When flour is cooked (it turns brown), add cream and bring to a boil over a lower flame; simmer.
3) Stir in cheese until it is completely melted. Season with salt and pepper. If sauce seems too thick, thin it out by adding a little more cream.

Chicken Supreme

This sauce is almost the same as our Brown Sauce except that it's made only for chicken dishes. Because of this, we'll use a chicken base instead of a beef base. I will also revert back to this page in the next chapter, for there will be several recipes that call for the yumminess of this supreme sauce.

INGREDIENTS

- 1 can *College Inn*® chicken broth
- 1 pint heavy cream
- ½ stick butter
- ¼ cup all-purpose flour
- ¼ cup cooking sherry
- pinch of thyme
- pinch of parsley, finely chopped
- pinch of salt and pepper

PREPARATION

1) Melt butter in medium saucepan; add flour, and cook roux until flour taste is gone.
2) Add sherry, mix well with wooden spoon.
3) Add chicken broth and cream.
4) Use whisk to mix sauce; add all dried herbs and spices, simmer over a low flame for 15-20 minutes.
4) Strain through sieve to remove any bits of flour— the ideal sauce should come out velvety smooth after straining.

GARRY'S GOODS

When you freeze and then defrost sauce, it tends to become watery. Adding a half can of tomato paste while you're heating it up as a leftover should solve that problem.

3^{50}

For marinara madness

1½ hours

1 quart

Marinara Sauce

This classic tomato sauce can't go wrong and can be used in over a hundred dishes! I'll give you the recipes for a lot of dishes to be made using this wonderful sauce in the "Main Course" chapter. It has no meat ingredients, so if you're a vegetarian— this is the sauce for you.

I N G R E D I E N T S

- ¼ cup olive oil
- 8-ounce can *Del Monte*® tomato sauce
- 28-ounce can *Tuttarosa*® crushed tomatoes
- 3 cloves garlic, chopped
- 1 carrot, peeled and finely chopped
- ¼ cup parsley, finely chopped
- ½ cup fresh basil, washed and finely chopped
- 1 medium onion, peeled
- ¼ cup red wine

P R E P A R A T I O N

1) In a large saucepan, heat oil and add garlic, stirring with wooden spoon— do not burn garlic.
2) Add carrot, parsley, and basil. Next, add wine and simmer for 10-15 minutes.
3) Add crushed tomatoes and tomato sauce; drop in the whole onion. (This may seem gross but you'll remove it when the sauce is done.)
4) This sauce should cook for 1 to 1½ hours on a very low flame (simmer).

Meat Sauce

This has the same culinary basis as the Marinara Sauce except it contains meat. Pork chops and meatballs are usually served with "Sunday sauce"– properly named because it's what traditional Italians eat up every Sunday with their family. So, if you're away from your family for any length of time *(especially* if you're of Italian descent), there's no doubt in my mind that you'll long for the smell of a good meat sauce simmering through your nasal passageways.

I N G R E D I E N T S

- 1 pound pork chops, brasciole, or any other gravy meat
- Same ingredients as Marinara Sauce (at left)

P R E P A R A T I O N

You will be making this exactly as the Marinara Sauce recipe on the previous page, except that after you add the garlic, carrot, and herbs, add your meat and brown it. After that, add wine, tomato product, and finally the onion.

My suggestion is to cook this sauce as long as you can– obviously the longer the better. Always remember to simmer on a low flame. I would say minimum cooking time is an hour and a half. Serve it with your favorite pasta and invite the cool campus crowd.

GARRY'S GOODS

My dad always used to make this sauce the day before the "big day"! It tastes better this way!

$5
per quart

60-90 minutes

1 quart

SIDE D
'n SA

chapter 4

DISHES & SALADS

"These'll make your pals GREEN with envy!"

When creating your meal, it's always nice to start off with a salad, and have something to accompany your main course. For example— meat and potatoes... turkey and stuffing... antipasto and lasagna *(my personal favorite!)*.

Here are some simple side dishes to use. They're all great items to jazz up your main course. And, don't worry— I'll start you off with some specialized salads and work you up on to some other super side dishes!

GARRY'S GOODS

Caesar Salad

Hail Caesar! There are not too many people I know that *don't* like Caesar salad. Maybe if they found out what's in the dressing though, they may not be fans any longer. *Secret:* Anchovies happen to be one of the main ingredients but you don't have to put them in if you really despise them.

**Protein Alert:
Want to make a meal out of it? Grill two chicken cutlets, slice into strips, and mix with your salad– instant Chicken Caesar.**

I N G R E D I E N T S

- 1 head Romaine lettuce
- 1 cup croutons

DRESSING

- $\frac{1}{2}$ can anchovy filets in oil
- $\frac{1}{4}$ cup olive oil
- 2 cloves garlic
- 2 tablespoons mustard
- 1 egg yolk
- 1 lemon, juiced
- 1 tablespoon *Worcestershire®* sauce
- $\frac{1}{4}$ cup grated cheese

P R E P A R A T I O N

1) Wash lettuce very well, removing all dirt. Cut leaves into bite-sized pieces. Place in wooden salad bowl and set aside.
2) In blender or hand mixer, pour in all dressing ingredients and blend for 30 seconds.
3) Mix dressing and lettuce in bowl, tossing very well. Top off with croutons and sprinkle on extra grated cheese.

$2⁵⁰

per salad

50%

10 minutes

3-4 servings

Italian Salad

Here's one of those things you can make simple or throw
everything into. I prefer to do the throwing thing!
It's perfect to have if you invite the gang over
for a Spaghetti and Meatball dinner (pg. 70).

I N G R E D I E N T S

- 1 head Iceberg lettuce
- 1 head Romaine lettuce
- 3-4 plum tomatoes, sliced
- 1 small jar jardiniere salad or artichoke hearts
- 1 can black olives, sliced

DRESSING

- ½ cup olive oil
- ¼ cup balsamic vinegar
- ¼ cup garlic powder
- pinch of salt and pepper

P R E P A R A T I O N

1) Clean lettuce well and break apart. Slice tomato into
   round circles; drain liquid from jardiniere salad; drain
   liquid from olives.
2) Toss together and put in salad bowl.
3) Shake vinegar, oil, garlic powder, and salt
   and pepper.
4) Toss dressing and salad together. Eat up!

GARRY'S GOODS

*With this salad,
the sky is the limit...*
**The more you put into
it, the better it gets!
Don't be afraid to
enhance the greenery
of your meals— add
some salad savvy by
throwing in your
favorite cheeses
or cold cuts!**

$4-5
feeds all!

50%

15 minutes

68 people

$34
super servings

75%

15 minutes

34 servings

Spinach Salad

Hey, you either like spinach or you hate it. I like it and it's
good for you, too— I know this 'cause Popeye says so.

INGREDIENTS

- 1 package fresh spinach
- 2-3 strips bacon
- 2 hard boiled eggs

DRESSING

- 1/4 cup vegetable oil
- 1/4 cup mayonnaise
- 1/4 cup cider vinegar
- 1/8 cup bacon fat
- pinch of salt and pepper

PREPARATION

1) Clean spinach well and break apart.
2) Cook bacon in toaster oven until crispy
   (about 10-15 minutes).
3) Crumble bacon and chop egg into pieces; set aside.
4) In blender or hand mixer, combine all dressing
   ingredients, blend for 30 seconds.
5) Toss dressing with spinach, top with bacon bits
   and egg.

Mozzarella and Tomato Salad with Fresh Basil

This dish is a wonderful way to start off a nice Italian meal. It's also *molto simplice* (Italian for "very easy") to prepare and is a perfect first course when cooking for that special someone.

I N G R E D I E N T S

- 1 piece mozzarella, preferably fresh
- 2 large beefsteak tomatoes
- 1 bunch fresh basil
- $\frac{1}{4}$ cup olive oil
- $\frac{1}{8}$ cup balsamic vinegar
- pinch of garlic powder
- pinch of salt and pepper

P R E P A R A T I O N

1) Slice mozzarella in $\frac{1}{4}$-inch round slices. Slice tomato in the same way, removing core.
2) On a small plate, place a slice of mozzarella, then a slice of tomato, and continue to fill the plate— mozzarella, tomato, mozzarella, tomato, etc..
3) Clean basil well, pull off leaves, and arrange on top of tomato and mozzarella.
4) In a small mixing bowl, combine oil, vinegar, garlic, salt and pepper; mix well. Drizzle dressing on top of salad and serve.

GARRY'S GOODS

If you can get fresh mozzarella for this one, I totally recommend it.

$4.5 for both insalade

0%

10 minutes

2 servings

$2

lots of noodle noshin'

0%

10 minutes

4-6 people

German Style Buttered Noodles

Here's a side dish my mom used to make. It goes great with all poultry and meat dishes, especially ones that have a sauce, like stews and casseroles. The key to this one is to drop a bouillon cube into the water when boiling the noodles, and only put in enough water to cover the noodles up. When the noodles are soft, there should only be a minimal amount of liquid left— it's this liquid that helps to flavor the noodles.

INGREDIENTS

- 1-pound package wide egg noodles
- 2 bouillon cubes, beef or chicken
- 1/4 cup dried parsley flakes
- 1/2 stick butter

PREPARATION

1) Boil water in a pot big enough to hold a package of noodles. When water comes to a rolling boil, drop in bouillon cubes and noodles, stir constantly.

3) In about seven minutes, test noodles for desired done-ness (my word!), remove from heat. There should only be enough liquid left to keep noodles moist. If there is more than that, pour some of the liquid out— we want them moist, not soupy.

4) Next, add butter and parsley flakes. That's it!

Oven Roasted Potatoes

Here's an easy side dish that goes real well with Roasted Chicken (pg. 66) or any roast for that matter. The good part is that if you prep it ahead of time, it'll cook in about the same amount of time as your roast.

If you want to speed up the process, give the potatoes a boil ahead of time— this will cut down on the time it'll take to bake 'em up.

I N G R E D I E N T S

- 5-6 Idaho baking potatoes, scrubbed well– do not peel!
- ¼ cup oil
- 1 clove garlic, chopped
- pinch of thyme
- pinch of rosemary
- pinch of parsley
- pinch of salt and pepper

P R E P A R A T I O N

1) Wash potatoes well under running water, remove eyes if there are any (not *your* eyes, the potatoes' eyes). Cut lengthwise, and then cut them again until you have quartered 'tators. Dry them well.
2) Heat oil in frying pan. When hot, add garlic and brown it. Next, add potatoes and give them a quick sauté. When potatoes get some color, add herbs and spices.
3) Transfer to a heat-proof casserole dish or baking pan and bake at 375° for 35-40 minutes or until fork tender.

potato paradise

0%

30 minutes

4 pals

GARRY'S GOODS

If your rice is too soggy, place a piece of bread on top and close the lid– this will absorb excess moisture.

$2⁵⁰
For it all!

0%

25-30 minutes

4 pilaf pals

Rice Pilaf

Another perfect companion to a hearty meal is rice–
especially if *your* perfect companion is beside you!
This can be served with poultry, beef, fish, or shellfish.
It's basically just a variation to regular white rice.
Depending on what you might be making,
I'd recommend that you use that same type
of stock (chicken or beef) to flavor your pilaf.

INGREDIENTS

- 1½ cups *Uncle Ben's Converted Rice®*
- 2 cans *College Inn®* chicken or beef broth
- 1 medium onion, finely chopped
- 1 cup mushrooms, sliced (optional)
- ¼ cup fresh parsley, chopped
- ½ stick butter
- ⅛ cup oil

PREPARATION

1) Melt butter and oil in medium saucepan. When hot, add onions and sauté until clear.
2) Add rice, sauté with butter, oil, and onion. Mix well with wooden spoon. When rice begins to get color, add broth. (Liquid should cover rice by about 1-2 inches; if this does not occur, add a little water.)
3) Add mushrooms if you desire (otherwise skip it); add parsley. Cover and simmer for approximately 20 minutes or until rice is soft and puffy. Season to taste.

Stuffing

My favorite part of Thanksgiving isn't the turkey, but the stuffing. Not everyone makes stuffing the same way, and to be honest with you– it *can* be a chore. But, if you really want to impress his or her folks with your culinary know-how, read on– then stuff it!

I N G R E D I E N T S

- 1 bag herb-flavored stuffing
- 1 large onion, finely diced
- 1-2 cloves garlic, finely diced
- 2-3 sweet Italian sausage links
- 1 can *College Inn*® chicken broth
- 1 teaspoon poultry seasoning
- 1 stick butter
- 1 egg
- ¼ cup oil

P R E P A R A T I O N

1) In a large saucepan, melt butter and add oil. When hot, add onion and garlic, sauté.
2) Add sausage meat and brown (this takes about 15 minutes); add broth and stuffing a little at a time, stirring with wooden spoon. Consistency should be that of "lumpy mashed potatoes." If it's not, adding a little hot water will do the trick. If it's too watery, add more stuffing.
3) Remove from heat and cool for about 10 minutes. Add egg to bind it. Eat up or get ready to stuff your bird– follow cooking instructions that come on the turkey's outside wrapping.

GARRY'S GOODS

With this one, I suggest an Oven Stuffer Roaster. You'll be able to have the holidays any time you please!

$3-4
super stuffing

50%

30 minutes

4-6 pals

MAIN C

chapter
5

OURSE

This is where you can really put on a big show in the kitchen– or corner of your dorm room deemed as such. You made it through the *Munchies,* the *Soups* and *Sauces,* then the *Side Dishes 'n Salads*– finally, the moment we've all been waiting for: *The Main Event!*

You may not even want to go beyond the Munchies section, but hey, let's face it– you're in school, your work is done for the weekend, the weather stinks, you're sitting around hanging out, doing nothing– when is there a *more perfect time* for a FOOD FEST?!

Chip in with some pals and make a big pot of sauce and some meatballs, or a delicious shrimp scampi... heck, show off and invite the whole dorm! Anything is better than cafeteria food!

Remember– "the way to a man's heart is through his stomach..." and "the way to a woman's heart is through romance." There is nothing more romantic than cooking dinner for that special someone in your life. If that person hasn't gotten to be that special someone yet, cooking dinner for him or her *may* seal your fate. Good food, some candles, and soft music... beats Mickey D's any day! As always, I wish you luck.

GARRY'S GOODS

When you're stirring, try to get everything that is stuck to the bottom of the pot off. The little particles of flour and what-not have a tendency to burn and could ruin your stew.

$6 per bowl

50%

30 minutes

4-6 persons

Beef Stew

Here's a great dish for a cold day. And, the best part about it is that once you get it going, you really don't have to pay too much attention to it— the longer it cooks, the better. In addition, in order to keep Mom happy, it contains all the major food groups, and is even better as a leftover.

INGREDIENTS

- 1 medium-sized top round, London Broil, cubed
- 3-4 Idaho potatoes, peeled and cubed
- 3-4 carrots, peeled and sliced into circles
- 2 medium onions, cubed
- 1 can *College Inn*® beef broth
- 1 cup flour
- ¼ cup oil
- ¼ cup fresh parsley, chopped
- pinch of thyme
- pinch of salt and pepper

PREPARATION

1) Heat oil in large saucepan with a tight fitting lid.
2) Pour flour into a deep dish and season with salt and pepper.
3) Carefully flour each piece of meat, shaking off excess flour; put directly in hot oil and brown.
4) When every piece of meat has been browned on both sides, add your vegetables, parsley, and thyme. Give a stir with a wooden spoon and add beef broth.
5) Keep stirring until all of the broth has been absorbed— if it looks too pastey, add some water (a cup or so will do).
6) Simmer on a very low flame for a minimum of an hour. Every 10-15 minutes, give it a stir.

Chicken á la King

This is basically the inside of chicken pot pie— the best part, I say! The main reason why this recipe is "king" (aside from its great taste), is that it's exceptionally easy to make and is very cost efficient. And, if you want to "kill two chickens with one stone," make yourself Chicken Soup (pg. 29), remove chicken from soup, boil up a couple of breasts, dice the chicken— you'll have yourself some instant chicken soup *and* chicken á la king.

I N G R E D I E N T S

- 2 cups cooked chicken meat, diced
- 1 package frozen mixed vegetables
- 1 cup Chicken Supreme Sauce (pg. 46)
- ¼ cup fresh parsley, chopped

P R E P A R A T I O N

1) If you choose not to make the chicken soup but want to make the á la king, boil up 2-3 chicken breasts, cool, and dice into cubes.
2) Steam the mixed vegetables over low heat by putting them in a pot, throwing in a cup of water, and simmering for 10 minutes or so. When cooked, drain off all excess liquid.
3) Prepare Chicken Supreme Sauce (pg. 46); add diced chicken and mixed vegetables, simmer for 10 minutes.
4) Season and garnish with chopped parsley.

GARRY'S GOODS

I highly recommend making the Rice Pilaf (pg. 57) with this dish.

$3
per person

0%

25 minutes

3.5 happy buds

Chicken Francais

If you really want to impress your other half, this lemon chicken dish is the one to make. It looks complicated, it sounds complicated, but in reality, it's quite simple.

INGREDIENTS

- 1 package chicken cutlets, thinly sliced
- 3 eggs
- ¼ cup olive oil
- ¼ stick butter
- 1 lemon
- ¼ cup white wine
- 1 can *College Inn*® chicken broth
- 1 cup all-purpose flour
- ½ cup grated cheese
- ¼ cup fresh parsley
- pinch of salt and pepper

PREPARATION

1) Beat eggs and parsley in a small mixing bowl. Mix flour, cheese, salt and pepper in another bowl.
2) Heat oil and butter in a frying pan. Take a small dab of egg on the tip of your finger and put it in the hot oil– if it rises to the top, you're ready to sauté.
3) Dredge the cutlets in the flour mixture and completely coat them, shake off excess.
4) Dip floured cutlets in egg and sauté in saucepan. When both sides get golden brown, remove and transfer to a plate. Do this with all cutlets.
5) Add white wine to butter and oil in pan– this is called de-glazing. Completely squeeze juice from lemon into pan (minus the seeds, of course!).
6) Add chicken broth to pan and bring to a boil. Reduce heat, put cutlets back in pan, and cook for five more minutes.
7) Lay cutlets on plate, spoon sauce on top, sprinkle with a little chopped parsley, and dig in!

Chicken Marsala

Here is another impressive meal that also looks more complicated than it actually is. You will need a sweet wine called Marsala for this recipe— you can find it in most liquor stores; supermarkets also carry it.

I N G R E D I E N T S

- 1 package chicken cutlets, thinly sliced
- 1/2 pound white button mushrooms, sliced
- 1/2 cup flour
- 1/4 cup olive oil
- 1/2 stick butter
- 1/4 cup fresh parsley
- 1/4 cup Marsala wine
- 1 lemon, juiced
- 1 can *College Inn®* beef broth
- pinch of salt and pepper

P R E P A R A T I O N

1) Heat oil and butter in a frying pan. Season flour with salt and pepper.
2) Dredge cutlets through the flour and sauté. When both sides are golden brown, transfer all cutlets to a plate.
3) Add mushrooms to pan and sauté. While the mushrooms are being sautéed, add Marsala wine, lemon, and beef broth. Transfer cutlets back to pan and simmer over a low flame for 5-10 minutes. Season and plate.

GARRY'S GOODS

A nice pot of spaghetti and Marinara Sauce (pg. 47) goes best with this Italian classic.

$3⁵⁰

the whole parmigiana

20%

25 minutes

2-3 friends

Chicken Parmigiana

"Here's a lovely way to end-a' you day." Once you have your Marinara Sauce made (pg. 47), the rest is easy.

INGREDIENTS

- 1 package chicken cutlets, thinly sliced
- 2 eggs
- ½ cup flour
- 1 cup *4-C Seasoned Italian Breadcrumbs®*
- ½ cup olive oil
- 2 cups Marinara Sauce (pg. 47)
- 1 package sliced mozzarella or muenster cheese
- pinch of parsley
- pinch of salt and pepper

PREPARATION

1) Beat eggs in small mixing bowl. In a separate bowl, mix flour, salt and pepper. Dump some seasoned breadcrumbs in yet another bowl.
2) Heat oil in frying pan, take a dab of egg on your finger, and put it in the oil (the egg, *not* your finger!). When the egg floats to the top, you're ready to fry.
3) Dredge cutlets in flour, egg, and breadcrumbs.
4) Fry these up on both sides until golden brown; transfer cutlets to a paper towel to absorb grease.
5) When all cutlets are done, preheat oven to 350°, put cutlets on a baking sheet, cover with sauce and piece of cheese. Bake up for 10 minutes.

Roasted Chicken

Nothing could be easier than roasting a chicken, as long as you have an oven large enough to roast one in. Even if you can't cook this one up at college, imagine the look on your parents' faces if you tackle their kitchen with this one!

I N G R E D I E N T S

- 2½- to 3-pound chicken
- ¼ cup olive oil
- 2-3 cloves fresh garlic, finely chopped
- pinch of thyme
- pinch of rosemary
- ¼ cup fresh parsley
- pinch of paprika
- pinch of salt and pepper

P R E P A R A T I O N

1) Preheat oven to 375°. Wash chicken well. Remove gizzard bag inside the cavity, dry, and set aside.
2) In a small mixing bowl, combine all listed ingredients except the chicken.
3) Place chicken on a roasting pan, preferably one with a drip rack. Take your mixture and brush evenly over chicken and inside cavity.
4) Place chicken on rack in center of oven and bake at 375° for approximately 50 minutes. A good way to test for done-ness is to stick a fork in the leg joint; if juices run clear, your chicken is done.

GARRY'S GOODS

Any of the side dishes listed in Chapter 4 are perfect to side serve with this. In my opinion, the Stuffing (pg. 58) is the best, and the Chicken Supreme Sauce (pg. 46) is excellent on top.

$5
the whole roast

50%

60 minutes

3-6 pals

GARRY'S GOODS

Make sure your Marinara Sauce (pg. 47) is made ahead of time for this one.

$8
For Four-cheese fun

25%

30 minutes

6-8 buddies

Four Cheese Baked Macaroni

This dish is great for a group, or you can make it and have leftovers all to yourself for days. What's best is to get together with some friends, chip in, and make it like a Sunday-afternoon-watching–the–games-on–TV kinda' thing. You'll need either a disposable aluminum roasting pan or a baking pan for this dish.

INGREDIENTS

- 2 1-pound boxes *Ronzoni®* ziti or penne
- 1½ quarts Marinara Sauce (pg. 47)
- 1-pound package mozzarella and provolone cheese, shredded
- 1-pound container ricotta cheese
- 1 whole egg
- ¼ cup romano cheese, grated
- ¼ cup fresh parsley, chopped

PREPARATION

1) Boil macaroni as directed. Drain, rinse, and transfer back to the pot.
2) Mix macaroni with half the sauce, mozzarella, provolone, and romano cheese.
3) Add egg and ricotta; mix well.
4) Put some sauce on bottom of baking dish so *macs* don't stick. Pour macaroni mixture on top of that.
5) When all of the macaroni is in baking dish, top with the rest of the sauce and then the rest of the cheeses. Sprinkle with the parsley and bake up at 375° for about 30-45 minutes or until top is golden brown and bubbly.

Lasagna

This is similar to the baked macaroni recipe.
It feeds a few friends, you make it in bulk, and it
tastes much better the next day. In fact, my suggestion
is make this one on Saturday for Sunday munchin'.
Again, you'll need Marinara Sauce and
a medium baking pan for this delicacy.

I N G R E D I E N T S

- 1 package *No Boil*® lasagna sheets
- 1½ quarts Marinara Sauce (pg. 47)
- 1 egg
- 1 package mozzarella cheese, shredded
- 1-pound container ricotta cheese
- ¼ cup romano cheese
- ¼ cup fresh parsley, chopped
- pinch of salt and pepper

P R E P A R A T I O N

1) In a medium mixing bowl, combine half the
   mozzarella, all the ricotta and romano cheese, egg,
   salt and pepper; mix well then set aside.
2) Coat bottom of baking pan with a thin layer of
   Marinara Sauce; top with one layer of lasagna; cover
   with another thin layer of sauce.
3) Top sauce with the cheese mixture and another thin
   layer of sauce; follow with another lasagna sheet.
4) Repeat this process until there's only about a half-inch
   remaining at the top of the pan.
5) Top off with remaining sauce and cheeses, sprinkle
   with parsley, and bake at 350° for 45 minutes or until
   top is bubbly.

GARRY'S GOODS

There are many types
of lasagna. For
Vegetable Lasagna,
sauté up some sliced
zucchini, broccoli,
carrots, and yellow
squash and add to
your cheese mixture.
Or how about a Meat
Lasagna for all you
carnivores? Throw
some sautéed sausage
and ground beef into
your marinara sauce.

$8
per pan

50%

30-45 minutes

4-6 lasagna lovers

GARRY'S GOODS

I highly recommend serving this up with the Brown Sauce (pg. 44) and instant mashed potatoes. The German Style Noodles (pg. 55) also make a nice accompaniment.

$7
per loaf

50%

45 minutes

4 pals

Meatloaf

I used to despise Meatloaf until I came upon a recipe for my mighty meatballs. I have to admit, I make some darn good meatballs— so I said to myself: "If a meatball is only a small version of a Meatloaf, what the heck— let's see if it works!" And "shiver me timbers and blow me down"– it did! You'll need a bread loaf tin for this.

INGREDIENTS

- 1 pound fresh ground beef
- 1 pint heavy cream or half & half
- 4 slices white bread, cut into pieces
- 1 egg
- 1 small onion, finely chopped
- ¼ cup ketchup
- 1-2 cloves garlic, finely chopped
- ¼ cup fresh parsley, chopped
- pinch of thyme
- pinch of salt and pepper

PREPARATION

1) Beat egg and cream in a medium mixing bowl; add bread and soak.

2) Add ground beef, chopped onion, garlic, parsley, salt, pepper, and thyme. Mix well until mixture comes off the side of bowl easily. If it seems too watery, add some bread crumbs to tighten it up.

3) Spray bottom of bread tin with *Pam®;* transfer mixture into tin and mold into a loaf. Cover top with ketchup and bake for 30 minutes at 375° or until the top browns.

Spaghetti and Meatballs

Ya' can't get much simpler than this— it takes almost no time at all to make!

INGREDIENTS

- 2 1-pound boxes of *Ronzoni®* spaghetti
- 1 quart Marinara Sauce (pg. 47) or Meat Sauce (pg. 48)
- 1 pound fresh ground beef
- 1 pint half & half or heavy cream
- 1 whole egg
- 4 slices white bread, cut into pieces
- 1-2 cloves garlic, finely chopped
- 1/4 cup grated cheese
- 1/4 cup fresh parsley, chopped
- pinch salt and pepper

PREPARATION

1) Boil spaghetti in large pot, stirring constantly so it doesn't stick.
2) For meatballs, follow same preparation as Meatloaf (at left), except instead of making a loaf, roll them into balls about one inch in diameter. Bake them up at 375° for 15 to 20 minutes.
3) Drain pasta with colander, transfer back to pot, and cover with sauce. Serve with meatballs and grated cheese.

GARRY'S GOODS

Meatball Parmigiana Hero sound interesting? All you need to do is melt some cheese on top of your meatballs, put it on Italian bread, and "mangia"!

$6 per pot

50%

30 minutes

4-6 hungry buds

GARRY'S GOODS

This is a low-fat recipe. If you really want to let your hair down and make the recipe a little more rich, substitute one stick of butter for the oil. Then, after all the veggies are added, stir in a pint of heavy cream, add cheese, and viola! It'll be enough to literally stick to your ribs!

$1²⁵

per primavera pal

50%

25 minutes

4 plates

Pasta Primavera

Your momma would be proud. This one has all your veggies and pasta in one meal. Remember– the more veggies, the merrier! Feel free to delete or add to your liking. Here's my suggested recipe.

INGREDIENTS

- 1 box pasta of your choice: ziti, penne, rigatoni, fettuccini
- 3 tablespoons olive oil
- 4-5 pieces of garlic, finely chopped
- 1/4 cup parmesan cheese
- 1/4 cup fresh parsley, chopped
- 1 small onion, finely chopped (or 2 scallions)
- 1 green zucchini, cut in 1/2 moons
- 1 yellow zucchini, cut in 1/2 moons
- 1/2 cup frozen peas
- 1 red or orange pepper, julienne
- 1 package frozen broccoli florets

PREPARATION

1) In a large saucepan fill up three quarters to the top with warm tap water and bring to a boil.
2) When water reaches a boil, add macaroni and stir. Cook to desired tenderness (about 10 minutes).
3) When cooked, strain and run under cold water; set aside.
4) In a frying pan, heat oil, add garlic, brown lightly.
5) Add onion, zucchini, pepper, broccoli, and peas. Stir constantly until veggies start to soften.
6) At desired tenderness, add macaroni and stir 'til macs get hot.
7) Sprinkle with parmesan cheese and fresh parsley.

Shrimp Scampi

I saved the best for last! I don't know how many of you like seafood, but those who do usually enjoy eating shrimp very, very much! This one is fairly easy to make and is a nice dish to serve on that romantic occasion, or if you just want to impress the heck out of someone! (Sorry, you *can't* bring it along on a job interview!)

I N G R E D I E N T S

- 1 pound of shrimp, peeled, cleaned, and de-veined
- 2-3 cloves fresh garlic, finely chopped
- ½ stick butter, cut into pieces
- ¼ cup white wine
- ¼ cup *4C Italian Seasoned Breadcrumbs*®
- 2 tablespoons parmesan cheese, grated
- ¼ cup fresh parsley, chopped

P R E P A R A T I O N

1) If you <u>"skeeve"</u> (See *Goods* for a "New Yawker" translation!) peeling shrimp, you may be able to ask the guy in the fish store to do it for you. In either case, they should be cleaned well; all of the shells must be removed to avoid choking to death.
2) Place shrimp in baking pan, cover with chopped garlic, butter, and wine; sprinkle top with grated cheese, breadcrumbs, and parsley. Bake at 375° for 10-15 minutes and serve.

GARRY'S GOODS

New Yawker Translation: "skeeve": gross out, disgusting, yuck, despicable, don't-touch-it-with-a-10-foot-pole, ugh, abominable, eek... (you get the picture).

scampi city!

0%

15-20 minutes

4-6 shrimp "scampers"

DESS

chapter
6

ERTS

Lots of words have been associated with dessert– sinful, heavenly, dreamy, luscious, orgasmic, sweet, sultry, and decadent. Sounds kinda' like a trashy novel if you ask me.

For some, dessert is the whole point of a meal... you look more forward to the end of the meal than the rest of it. (*Not me*, of course!)

Whatever the case may be, I think there's nothing better than finishing off a nice, homemade meal with a dessert that's homemade– it puts the topping on the cake, literally!

With the recipes to follow, I have replaced the Gas Probability Factor (*by now, who cares!*) with the Fattening Factor. I've done my best to keep these desserts as low-cal as possible. I also offer up some sidebar tips on how to substitute fatty ingredients with healthier, nutritional ones that still keep the dishes delectable and scrumptious. Enjoy!

GARRY'S GOODS

Nothing beats pie á la mode. A scoop of cold ice cream on top is quite yummy. For a really healthy substitute, frozen yogurt is just as delicious with a lot less fat and calories!

$2⁵⁰

for the crumble

fat face

35 minutes

1 pie

French Crumb Apple Pie

In the fall, apples are quite plentiful, especially if you attend an eastern college or one in the upstate New York, New Jersey, or Washington area. Best of all, they're cheap! So, on that cold Autumn day, fire up the oven and bake a pie just like grandma used to. It's as easy as (sorry...) pie!

INGREDIENTS

- 5-6 medium Macintosh or Delicious apples
- 1 frozen pie shell
- 1 cup brown sugar
- 1 small package raisins
- ½ cup water
- ¼ cup flour
- 1 stick butter
- 2 tablespoons cinnamon
- 1 teaspoon nutmeg
- 2 tablespoons corn starch

PREPARATION

1) Preheat oven at 350°
2) Prick the bottom of the pie shell with a fork and pre-bake it for five minutes. Remove and set aside.

THE FILLING -
1) Peel and slice apples.
2) In a saucepan, melt half the butter.
3) Add apples and cook on low flame.
4) When apples start to get tender, add water, raisins, cinnamon, nutmeg, and half the brown sugar. Mix well; turn down the flame.
5) In a cup, add hot water to corn starch and make a paste; add to apple mixture– this will make a syrup.
6) Cook for five minutes then let cool.

THE TOPPING -
1) In a mixing bowl, combine the rest of butter, brown sugar, and flour– mix with a wooden spoon until it turns "crumbly."

THE PIE -
1) Add apple mixture to the shell, fill to the top, and sprinkle topping on the pie.
2) Bake for 20-25 minutes at 350° or until golden brown.

Baked Apples

Ah yes, back to the basics– you can't get much easier than this. And, getting back to the apple supply, when they're plentiful, *they're* plentiful!

I N G R E D I E N T S

- 4 Macintosh or Baking apples, unpeeled
- ½ cup brown sugar
- ¼ cup cinnamon
- ½ stick butter
- 1 cup water

P R E P A R A T I O N

1) Core the apples and remove all seeds. Be sure to do your coring without breaking though the apple's bottom.
2) Place on a greased baking sheet.
3) Cut butter in four equal portions and put a piece in the hole of each apple. Divide the sugar and cinnamon up equally and add to the apple.
4) Sprinkle some water on top of each apple for good measure– roughly a tablespoon each; bake at 350° for 15 minutes. Remove from oven and eat.

GARRY'S GOODS

Ice Box Cake

Oh boy, am I going to excite you with this one! It's quick, it's cheap, it's not fattening, and best of all– it's great!

INGREDIENTS

- 1 disposable pound cake aluminum tin
- 1 cup graham cracker crumbs
- 1 package *Jell-O Instant Chocolate Pudding*®
- *Cool Whip*® topping

PREPARATION

1) Line bottom of tin with graham cracker crumbs (save some for later!).
2) Mix pudding as per package instructions.
3) Pour pudding over crumbs.
4) Add reserved crumbs on top.
5) Refrigerate for an hour.
6) Remove and serve with *Cool Whip*®.

Experiment...
You don't have to use only chocolate pudding. There's lots of varieties of pudding out there... mix and match, use the low-fat ones, or add 'em all together for an Ice Box Surprise!

ice happiness!

thin face

10 minutes

1 cake

Brownies

Oh yeah... my favorite sinful dessert– home-baked brownies are phat! It doesn't get much better than this. And, they're pretty easy– just pay attention!

I N G R E D I E N T S

- 2 sticks sweet butter
- 4 ounces unsweetened chocolate
- 4 eggs
- 2 cups granulated sugar
- ½ cup unbleached all-purpose flour
- 1 teaspoon vanilla extract
- ⅔ cup shelled walnuts, chopped

P R E P A R A T I O N

1) Preheat oven to 350°. Grease and flour a 9 x 12 inch baking pan.
2) Melt butter and chocolate in the top part of a double broiler over boiling water. When melted, set aside to cool at room temperature (about 15 minutes.)
3) Beat eggs and sugar until thick and lemon-colored; add vanilla. Slowly add chocolate mixture to eggs and sugar; mix thoroughly.
4) Add flour gently to batter, mixing until blended. Add walnuts and mix well.
5) Pour into pan. Bake for 25 minutes or until center is set.
6) Allow brownies to cool in pan for 30 minutes before cutting into bars.

GARRY'S GOODS

Fruity!
Fresh strawberries or blueberries are great on this. If you don't want the fat and caloric content, substitute the cream cheese with a fat-free one. I'm telling ya' right now, though— I'm not taking any responsibility for that decision— I prefer the real thing, baby!

$5
per pie

fat face

45-60 minutes

1 pie

Easy Cheesecake

If you want to impress– this is the dessert to do it with!

INGREDIENTS

- 1 ready-made graham cracker crust pie shell
- 3 eggs, lightly beaten
- 2 cups sour cream
- 3 8-ounce packages of cream cheese at room temperature
- 1 cup granulated sugar
- ½ teaspoon salt
- 2 teaspoons vanilla extract

PREPARATION

1) Preheat oven to 375°.
2) Make your filling in a large mixing bowl; combine eggs, sour cream, cream cheese, eggs, salt, and sugar; blend until smooth with hand blender.
3) Bake cheesecake for 50 minutes; remove and cool.

Chocolate Chip Cookies

Picture this scenario: It's snowing, the wind is blowing, studying is boggling your brain, you're having a chocolate conniption, and you're just about bored to tears. What to do? Bake cookies! Call friends and make some hot cocoa. Want the recipe? Read on...

INGREDIENTS

- 1½ cups all-purpose flour
- 1 teaspoon baking soda
- 1 teaspoon ground cinnamon
- 2 sticks butter, softened
- 1 large egg
- 1 teaspoon vanilla extract
- 1½ cups old-fashioned rolled oats
- 1 cup semi-sweet chocolate chips

PREPARATION

1) Mix together flour, baking soda, and cinnamon.
2) Beat butter, brown sugar, and granulated sugar at medium speed with hand mixer until light and fluffy. Beat in egg and vanilla.
3) At low speed, beat in flour mixture until blended. Fold in oats and chocolate chips. Cover with plastic wrap and chill for one hour.
4) Preheat oven to 350°. Grease two baking sheets.
5) Shape dough into one-inch balls. Place cookies about two inches apart on prepared baking sheet. Flatten each cookie slightly.
6) Bake cookies until they are slightly browned around edges (about 10-12 minutes). Cool, then enjoy!

If you want your cookies warm and gooey again, just pop 'em in the microwave for 10 seconds on high. They're great with a tall glass of milk. It does a body good!

$6
per batch

fat face

25 minutes

4 dozen

FUN FOO

chapter

7

D FACTS

You know how great it is in the morning when you settle yourself in with a nice cup of OJ, a bowl of cereal, and the box propped up before ya'? You gotta' admit– the neatest facts were always revealed on the backs of those colorful boxes. Since our generation virtually grew up on such crunchy nuggets of news morsels, we've got a tremendous amount of appreciation for the sort.

This is why we've got our own brand of "back of book" knowledge. Read up on our *Fun Food Facts*... you're sure to learn lots. This way, when you ace one of our recipes, you'll be able to prop yourself up on your bunk, munch away, and learn tons! Hey– that's what college is for, right!?

Did You Know?

A HOT DOG ON YOUR TRAIL
Oscar Mayer has a "Wienermobile" that
travels on adventures around the country.

AIR MEAL MANIA
The first airline meal was available in 1919
when London and Paris travellers were able to buy
pre-packed meals on the plane for three shillings
(approximately seventy-five cents).

MAIL ORDER CAFFEINE MADNESS
Does your dorm coffee bring back visions of playing in
the mud? If so, you can order some yummy coffee beans
through the mail! The Roasters Select Coffee of the
Month Club offers a one- to two-pound coffee roast
specialty each month for only $9.95!
Call 800-JAVAS-2-U.

CHICKEN SOUP COMBATS A COLD
A recent study conducted by the University of
Nebraska Medical Center confirmed chicken
soup's ability to unclog nasal passages.

OREOS FOR THE 90s...
According to Oreo Fun Facts at *http://www.oreo.com*,
it takes 90 minutes to make each Oreo cookie
and every cookie contains 90 ridges.

PIZZA PIE TIME
The first pizzeria was established in
New York's Little Italy in 1905.

IT'LL FREEZE OUT THERE!

The first *Popsicle* came about by accident in 1923
when lemonade-mix salesman Frank Epperson
left a demonstration of his product on a windowsill
one cold winter's night. In the morning, the lemonade
had transformed into a chunk of yum.

DIET COKE IS ONLY A TEENAGER!

Diet Coke turned 15 in 1997–
it wasn't produced 'til 1982.

CASHIN' IN ON "FOOD TO GO"

Over $271.9 billion was spent on purchased
meals and beverages in 1995.

JIGGLIN' BIRTHDAY BABY!

Jell-O celebrated its 100th birthday in 1997!

THE "SACRED" BIG MAC

In keeping with the Hindu religion, there's a
beef-free *McDonald's* in India. Their equivalent
of a Big Mac is the Maharaj Mac, made of mutton.

HOLD THE TOMATO!

Believe it or not, the tomato was the slowest
food to catch on in Italy. Although the Aztecs
had already cultivated it by 1519, it took the
Italians more than a century before it came to be
used in their soups and sauces, and then another
century and a half before it was made into pasta sauce!

"YOU SAY POTATO, I SAY *BATATA*"

The first potato to arrive in Europe from its American homeland was not the normal french-fry kind, but a sweet potato brought over by Columbus in 1493, referred to by its Haitian name– *batata.*

WAITER, PLEASE!

Talk about setting the emperor's table...
up until 1492, the largest kitchen staff ever was at the court of the Ming Emperor of China. A total of 7,874 servants were needed to supply the imperial table and prepare state banquets.

"HAVE SOME SUGAR WITH YOUR RAIN..."

In 1969, the small town of Chester, South Carolina was plagued by periodic white showers whenever the town's non-dairy creamer plant's exhaust vents got clogged. That's right, non-dairy creamer rain showers splattered their homes and cars! Although the dairy sprinkles were harmless, they *were* messy. The company was ordered to pay the town $4,000 in 1991 to settle past damages. The problem causing these coffee-creamer "breaks" has since been resolved.

CASTLE OF CHAINS

Those greasily yummy *White Castle* boxes were around long before the *McDonald's* arches sprouted before our eyes every 10 blocks or so. The *White Castle* chain was the first burger franchise to stretch across America in 1921.

FROSTED FIRE!

A lawsuit brought on by an Ohio man paid $2,400 when he claimed a flaming *Pop-Tart* ignited his kitchen in 1995.

NO-COOK DESSERT
Twinkies® aren't baked! They are just sprayed into
a tube-shaped mold and left for a couple of hours.
So how *do* the bottoms get browned???

GETTIN' RID OF THOSE LEFTOVERS
Spam® was invented in 1937 as a way to use
up leftover pork shoulder. Since then, over
five billion cans have been sold.

FUNKY FUNGI
What do pompoms, straws, oysters, buttons,
and namekos have in common?
They are all types of mushrooms!

CELEBRITY VEGGIES
Among the growing number of vegetarians are some
famous figures, including Madonna, Oprah Winfrey,
Albert Einstein, Lisa Simpson (even cartoons are health
conscious!), David Duchovny, and Eddie Vedder.

QUICK HISTORY LESSON
Pasta was invented in China and
brought back to Italy by Marco Polo.

A CENTURY OF SOUP
Campbell's® Soups celebrate
their 100th birthday in 1997.

A HALF DECADE OF NUKIN'
The microwave oven turned 50 years old in 1997.

Cyber-Cool Cuisine

THE FOOD FRIENDLY WEB...

Check out *http://www.epicurious.com* to read
up on "Playing With Your Food", take part in
some fun food forums, and more!

RIB-LOVIN' GIRLS

Girls Who Eat Ribs at *http://www.gwer.com*
is an actual Web site that's a bucket combo
of hot & spicy and sweet & sour fun!

SEND YOUR FRIEND A CYBER-SANDWICH

Is your e-mail correspondence to pals lacking
a certain pizazz? If so, you might just need to
add a touch of mayo! *Best Foods®* mayo, that is!
From the company's Web site, properly nicknamed
Planet Sandwich, you can e-mail along a killer-sandwich
recipe at the click of a button. Check it out at
http://www.mayo.com/eastmayo/east.html.

HANDY KITCHEN TIPS

Hit this handy dandy, helpful site at
http://www.mcr. net/hotay/HKT/HKT-home.html
for quirky and quick kitchen tips, including how
to get a dropped egg mess off your floor.

DISNEY GIVEAWAY TRACKIN'

The *Disney* Fast Food Toys Picture Library at
http://www.mercury.hypersurf.com/~melchlo clues you
in on all those kids' meal giveaways from *McDonald's*,
Burger King, and other cool family fast food havens.
There's a site for *everything!*

CRACKIN' UP

You can find out almost anything you wish to know about crackers in a cyber-minute! Log onto "The Illustrated Guide To Crackers" at *http://www.netusa.net~eli/cstuff/index.html* and you'll see what we mean!

LID POPPER PAINS

This site is a terrifically tacky sales promotion aimed at those incapable few who are unable to open tightly sealed jars. If you're one of these people (or just want to check out what's available for those sad souls!), click on *http://dns.uttawa.net/~bbates/lidpopper.*

FEELING INVENTIVE?

If you're tired of the same ol' macaroni and cheese, you'll now be able to impress all your friends by learning how to make anything from "Bread & Butter Ice Box Pickles" to "Savory Zucchini Hotcakes." Find out how at *http://www.ksnw.com/recipes.*

"PEEP" SHOW

Remember those good ol' days at camp, roasting marshmallows around the fire? Well, this "peep" freak show demonstrates some sick trick spins on this once-pure, traditional activity. See it for yourself at *http://aris.sfrc.ufl.edu/~maryjo/peep_nuke/html.*

THE CYBER-FOOD LEADER

Our very own CollegeBound.NET at

http://www.cbnet.com

has many more of these enjoyable
Fun Food Facts, *Garry's Goods*,
Nutrition News, Cuisine Contests, and more!

The Scholarly Kitchen...

THE "FIRST YEAR" BLIMP...
The "freshman fifteen" is a term that describes
the typical amount of weight a freshman away
at college gains because of junk food bingin'!
Eat right and stay away!

HYATT HELP
Some of the nations' Hyatt Regency hotels offer
food and beverage internships where you can get
free meals, educational credits, and possibly
even full-time employment upon graduation!

COURSE COOKING
Culinary courses are offered by approximately
550 colleges and universities across the United States.

"A WHAT..?"
A *Rathskellar* is a small college cafeteria.
Not the most appetizing name for it, huh?!

CASHIN' IN ON SILVERWARE
Student internships at Oneida Foods in Boise, Idaho,
in the fields of marketing, packaging, and engineering
pay between $1,750 and $3,000 per month!

THEY WORK FOR FOOD
Food and beverage workers held
more than 4.5 million jobs in 1995.

ALL EMPLOYEES MUST WASH HANDS...

Important qualifications for chefs, cooks, and other kitchen workers are a keen sense of taste and smell, and meticulous personal cleanliness.

DELICIOUS CURRICULUM

The American Institute of Baking offers courses that include Pizza Production Technology, Principles of Corn Tortilla and Chip Production, and Bagels! Bagels! Bagels! That must be some yummy studying!

"I VANT TO STUDY YOUR FOOD"

At Transylvania University, in Lexington, Kentucky, (there *is* such a place!), you can learn the technique and procedure of quality food production in a real-life science lab. Such "experimentation" is open to those who major in Food Theory and Preparation.

DELICIOUS DEGREE

A Bachelor of Hamburgerology is awarded to graduates of *McDonald's* Hamburger University in Elk Grove, Illinois. All managers and owners must have one!

YUMMY MONEY

The Bakery, Confectionary and Tobacco Workers International Union offers eight scholarships per year to children of BC&TWIU members.

Nutrition News

CHEWING THE FAT...

Fat probably has the worst reputation of all diet items.
However, not *all* fat is bad for you. Those extra pounds
can be avoided if you know the different types of
fats and how much your body actually needs.
The worst fat is probably the one you're most familiar
with– the red meat, dairy, and greasy type known
as saturated fat. If you can learn to eat this
type of fat a little less, you'll be better off.

THIS MEANS:

Watching out for take-out food.

•

Staying away from anything fried.

•

Eating more fruits and vegetables
and less potato chips.

•

Trying to stay below 65 grams of fat a day.

•

Not falling into the fat-free trap.
Although these snack items have no fat,
they are usually high in sugar and
calories. Read the label!

CRASH COURSE IN CHOLESTEROL

You may think you're too young to worry about it,
but some of the foods you're eating now may be
causing your cholesterol level to skyrocket.

HERE ARE SOME THINGS
YOU SHOULD KNOW:

Cholesterol is that icky layer of
goo that aids in making hormones.
Too much of this stuff can build up around
your arteries and cause health problems.

•

A healthy diet where only eight to
10 percent of your daily caloric intake is from
saturated fat is a good start to help
lower your cholesterol.

•

A really good level is about 170.

•

Cholesterol Lowering Tips:
Greasy fries shouldn't be the staple meal
in your life; Try not to eat more than three
or four eggs a week; Instead of red meat,
opt for chicken and fish; Watch those
high-fat dairy products like whole milk
and cheese; Only use oil, butter,
and margarine in a limited manner.

<u>CALORIE COUNT</u>

The only thing most people know about calories
is that too many may keep us out of our favorite pair
of jeans. But calories are what give us the ability
to move and think– they are units of energy!
A healthy diet should consist of 2,000 calories a day.
That probably seems like it's a lot, right? Wrong!
The average meal at *McDonald's* can use up all
of these calories in a jiffy. The idea is to not only
limit caloric intake, but to make those calories count.

•

You may have noticed that most food nutrition
listings have a separate section for calories and
calories from fat. Your body naturally burns up
regular calories first, while leftover fat calories
are stored for later use. Love handles and chubby
thighs may be the result of too many leftover calories!

<u>BURN, BABY, BURN</u>

Foods high in sugar and fat are probably high
in calories, too. Be careful! Try to avoid the
wasteful calories in soft drinks and sugary juices–
water is the best substitute. Be aware of nutritional
labels, especially on junk food. Once you read 'em,
you may think twice before eating that second box of
cookies. Exercise and outdoor activities, such as
rollerblading and bike riding, use up lots of energy.
Get off that couch and start burning up those calories.

RECOMMENDED DAILY ALLOWANCES

	Men (ages 19-64)	Women (ages 19-64)
Vitamin A (microgms)	750	750
Thiamine (mg)	1.1	0.8
Riboflavin (mg)	1.7	1.2
Niacin (mg)	20	14
Vitamin B6 (mg)	2	1.4
Polate (mg)	200	200
Vitamin B12 (mg)	2	2
Vitamin C (mg)	40	50
Vitamin E (mg)	10	7
Zinc (mg)	12	12
Iron (mg)	7	12.6
Magnesium (mg)	320	270
Iodine (mg)	150	120
Calcium (mg)	800	800
Phosphorus (mg)	1000	1000
Selenium (mmol)	70	85
Sodium (mmol)	40-100	40-100
Potassium (mmol)	50-140	50-140

If you have cable TV, you may be lucky
enough to have the Food Network.
This 24-hour cooking show channel is
like an "all you can eat" TV fest! While
the main purpose of cooking shows is to
help ya' out in the kitchen, there are
some that are just fun to watch.
You may want to sample some of what
we think is very *tasteful* programming...

For more information about other
programs or schedules on the
Food Network, contact your local
cable operator or access them at
http://www.foodtv.com

• The Essence of Emeril

If you want to learn Louisiana/Cajun style cooking, this is definitely the show for you. Besides the creole recipes, what really adds *spice* to this show is the host himself, Emeril LaGosse. His hilarious stories and cool catch phrases, such as "kick it up a notch," are what add real *flavor* to the show.

• Ready, Set, Cook

Imagine that you are given an eggplant and told to make something out of it before your opponent does. That's the idea behind this combination game show/cooking show. This offbeat program pits cook against cook in a race to make the best dish. Master chefs and amateur contestants are *blended* together to create this scrumptious look at creative cooking.

• How to Boil Water

Just by the title of this show alone, one can tell that it uses a strange *ingredient* for a cooking show– comedy! In fact, *How to Boil Water* is hosted by stand-up comedian, Sean Donnellan. Besides water boiling, Sean guides his viewers through other simple recipes while keeping them laughing the whole time.

• Yan Can Cook

How many times did you wish that you knew how to make Chinese food favorites such as fried rice, spare ribs, and wonton soup? Well, our good friend Yan can teach you how to do just that! You're sure to learn why he has earned the title of "Fastest Cleaver in the West." You'll be amazed as he slices, dices, and chops with perfection.

Readin', Writin'

BOOKS

Are You Hungry Tonight? Elvis' Favorite Recipes
by Brenda Arlene Butler
(BLUEWOOD BOOKS, 1992)

Pasta Shmasta
by Karen Cross McKeown
(DOUBLEDAY BOOKS, 1995)

The Brilliant Bean
by Sally and Martin Stone
(BANTAM BOOKS, 1988)

Hog Wild
by K.C. McKeown
(WARNER BOOKS, 1992)

Curries Without Worries
by Sudha Koul
(WARNER BOOKS, 1993)

366 Healthful Ways To Cook Tofu
by Robin Robertson
(PLUME BOOKS, 1996)

Full of Beans
by Brooke Dojny
(HARPER PERENNIAL, 1996)

MAGAZINES

- Bon Appetit
- Chile Pepper
- Cook's Illustrated

and Munchin'

The California Pizza Kitchen Cookbook
by Larry Flax and Rick Rosenfield
(MACMILLAN PUBLISHING USA, 1996)

Simply Thai Cooking
by Wandee Young and Byron Ayanoglu
(ROBERT ROSE, INC., 1996)

Your Personal Nutritionist
by Ed Blonz, Ph.D.
(SIGNET, 1996)

Pasta E Verdura
by Jack Bishop
(HARPER COLLINS PUBLISHERS, 1996)

In the Kitchen With Miss Piggy
by Moi
(TIME-LIFE BOOKS, 1996)

The Everyday Cookbooks
(TIME-LIFE BOOKS, 1996)

Vegetarian Burgers
by Bharti Kirchner
(HARPER PERENNIAL, 1996)

Fresh and Fast
by Marie Simmons
(CHAPTERS PUBLISHING, LTD., 1996)

- Cooking Light: The Magazine of Food and Fitness
- Food and Wine
- Eating Well: The Magazine of Food and Health

A Food By Any

BANDS GOOD ENOUGH TO EAT...

- Bananarama
- Blind Melon
- Jimmy Buffet
- Kid Creole and the Coconuts
- Spice Girls
- Meat Puppets
- Cake
- The Cranberries
- Peaches & Herb
- Salt-n-Pepa
- Sugarcubes
- Ice Cube
- Veruca Salt
- Captain Beefheart
- Electric Prune
- 1910 Fruitgum Co.
- Hot Chocolate
- Ultimate Spinach
- The Honeydrippers
- Vic Chestnut
- Red Red Meat
- Green Jelly
- Pulp
- Country Joe & The Fish

- Chuck Berry
- Cream
- Ice-T
- Lemonheads
- John Mellencamp
- Mighty Lemon Drops
- Pearl Jam
- Fishbone
- Red Hot Chili Peppers
- The Smashing Pumpkins
- Vanilla Ice
- Lovin' Spoonful
- Blue Oyster Cult
- Lollipops
- Hot Tuna
- The Sugar Hill Gang
- Raspberries
- Moby Grape
- Fiona Apple
- Korn
- Coldcut/DJ Food/DJ Krush
- Hootie and the Blowfish
- Tangerine Dream
- Meat Beat Manifesto

Other Name...

MOVIE MUNCHIES...

- Like Water For Chocolate
- Kentucky Fried Movie
- Attack of the Killer Tomatoes
- What's Eating Gilbert Grape?
- Fried Green Tomatoes
- Nuts
- Looking For Mr. Goodbar
- The Pickle
- The Onion Field
- The Milagro Bean Wars
- Duck Soup
- Under A Cherry Moon
- Silence of the Lambs
- Clockwork Orange
- Breakfast At Tiffany's
- Milk Money
- Animal Crackers
- Mixed Nuts
- Children of the Corn
- Soul Food
- Good Burger
- Rumble Fish
- Strange Fruit
- Heartburn

- Hamburger Hill
- Hot Dog: The Movie
- James & the Giant Peach
- Meatballs
- Popcorn
- Mystic Pizza
- There's A Girl In My Soup
- The Apple Dumpling Gang
- The Life & Times of Judge Roy Bean
- Coconuts
- Cold Turkey
- Breakfast Club
- Bananas
- A Fish Called Wanda
- The Nutty Professor
- Space Jam
- Juice
- Who's Harry Crumb?
- Going Bananas
- The Spitfire Grill
- The Fisher King
- Deer Hunter
- Julius Caesar
- Eat, Drink, Man, Woman

FAMOUS FOOD NAMED CELEBS'

- Jack Lemon
- Meatloaf
- Christina Applegate
- Kevin Bacon
- Darryl Strawberry
- Olive Oyl
- Jimmy Crackcorn
- OJ Simpson
- Herb Albert
- Spud Webb
- Carrot Top
- Albert Cubby Broccoli
- Candy Bergen
- Peter Lemongello
- Onion Oreganto
- Ginger Rogers
- Chuck E. Cheese
- Alfalfa
- John Candy
- Esther Rolle

- Halle Berry
- Cheri Oteri
- Tea Leoni
- James Coco
- Brad Pitt
- Sweet Pea
- Tim Salmon
- Tim Rice
- Juice Newton
- Eve Plumb
- Sugar Ray Leonard
- Pepper Johnson
- Basil Rathbone
- Cookie Monster
- JJ Kale
- Bob Veal
- Buckwheat
- Farina
- Buster Crabb
- Napoleon

PLAY WITH YOUR FOOD!

- Gumby
- Strawberry Shortcake
- Bananas in Pajamas
- Candyland Bingo
- Hi Ho Cherry-O
- Thin Ice
- Hot Potato

- Cabbage Patch Kids
- Mr. Potatohead
- Pattycake
- Pickin' Chicken
- Go Fish
- Don't Spill The Beans
- Dominoes

TV DINNERS

- Chips
- Silver Spoons
- Huckleberry Hound
- Sesame Street
- Banana Splits

- Talk Soup
- Soupy Sails
- Mr. Bean
- Mr. Chips
- Lambchop

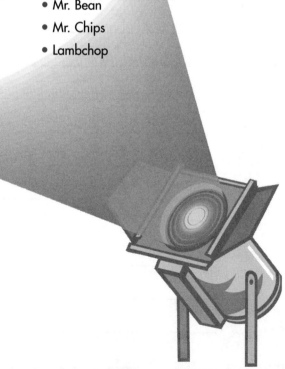

notes

notes

INDEX